THE AMERICAN DREAM BLUEPRINT

Your Ultimate Guide to US Citizenship

By
Nathan Venture, D

THE AMERICAN DREAM BLUEPRINT

Your Ultimate Guide to US Citizenship

CONTENTS

Introduction: Embarking on the Journey to Citizenship...................... 1

Chapter 1: The American Dream Blueprint: Your Ultimate Guide to US Citizenship... 4

Chapter 2: Understanding the Path to US Citizenship........................ 8
  Eligibility and Application Process 8
  Naturalization and the USCIS 9
  The Permanent Resident (Green Card) Gateway 12
  Other Paths: From Visas to Citizens 15

Chapter 3: The History of the United States...................................... 18
  The Founding Pillars 18
  From Colonization to Independence.. 21
  Expansion and Conflict: A Growing Nation 24

Chapter 4: Principles of American Democracy 28
  The Constitution and the Bill of Rights.. 28
  Federalism: The States and the Federal Government...................... 32
  The Rule of Law and the Role of the Courts.................................... 35

Chapter 5: The American Government Structure 39
  The Executive Branch: Powers and Responsibilities 40
  The Legislative Branch: Congress in Action 43
  The Judicial Branch: Interpreting the Law...................................... 46

Chapter 6: The Election Process and Citizenship 50
  Understanding Your Voting Rights.. 50
  Political Parties and the Electoral System 53
  The Importance of Civic Participation 56

Chapter 7: Rights and Responsibilities of Citizens 60
    Know Your Rights: Freedom and Protections 60
    Civic Duties and Responsibilities 63
    Community Contribution and Volunteering 66

Chapter 8: Important Symbols and Landmarks 70
    National Symbols and Their Meanings 71
    Historic Landmarks and Their Stories 73

Chapter 9: Insight into American Society 77
    Cultural Diversity and American Values 77
    Education and Work in the USA 80
    Social Issues and Public Opinion 84

Chapter 10: Economic Understanding: The US Market 87
    Basics of the American Economy 87
    The Role of Taxes and Personal Finance 90

Chapter 11: Preparing for the USCIS Civics Test 94
    Study Strategies and Resources 94
    Sample Questions and Answers 97
    Tips for Test Day Success 98

Chapter 12: The Interview and Beyond: Final Steps to Citizenship 101
    Mastering the Citizenship Interview 101
    The Oath of Allegiance Ceremony 104
    Life as a New US Citizen 107

Chapter 13: Keeping the Dream Alive: Continuous Learning 111
    Life-long Learning Opportunities 112
    Staying Informed and Engaged Citizen 115

Realizing the American Dream 118

Appendix A: Key Documents and Speeches in American History .. 121
    The Declaration of Independence (1776) 121
    The Constitution of the United States (1787) 121

The Bill of Rights (1791).. 122

The Federalist Papers (1787-1788)... 122

The Gettysburg Address (1863)... 122

Letter from Birmingham Jail (1963) 122

The Emancipation Proclamation (1863)... 123

Appendix B: Helpful Resources and Contact Information for
Immigrants 124

Government Resources 124

Educational Resources.. 125

Legal Assistance... 125

Community Support.. 125

Cultural Integration... 126

Motivation and Support.. 126

Appendix C: USCIS Civics Test Updates and Revisions 127

Understanding the Significance of Updates 127

Categories of Revisions... 127

Staying Informed 128

Embracing the Evolution 128

Glossary of Terms Related to US Citizenship 130

Online Review Request for This Book... 134

Introduction:
Embarking on the Journey to
Citizenship

Embarking on the journey towards becoming a U.S. citizen is a voyage filled with hopes, dreams, and aspirations. It's a pathway that promises the realization of achieving the American Dream, encompassed by the spirit of liberty, equality, and the pursuit of happiness. This journey is not just about acquiring a title or status but about integrating into the tapestry of one of the world's most diverse and dynamic societies.

The process of becoming a U.S. citizen is intricate and demands perseverance, dedication, and a profound understanding of the country's history, civic principles, and cultural nuances. It is more than a legal process; it's an embracing of American values and a commitment to contribute positively to the community and the nation at large.

In this guide, we embark on a comprehensive exploration of what it means to become a U.S. citizen. From understanding the procedural steps to delving into the rich historical context and civic responsibilities that citizenship entails, our aim is to provide a holistic view of the journey you are about to undertake.

The United States is a country built on the foundation of immigration, woven through centuries by the aspirations of those who came seeking a better life. This historical backdrop is not just a testament to the country's diversity but also its strength. As such, learning about the history of the United States is not just a requisite for citizenship; it's a way to connect with the spirit of those who have contributed to shaping this nation.

Understanding the principles of American democracy is vital. The Constitution, the Bill of Rights, and the federal structure form the backbone of the U.S. political system. Grasping these concepts will not only prepare you for the citizenship test but also equip you with the knowledge to actively participate in the democratic process.

The structure of the American government, with its checks and balances between the Executive, Legislative, and Judicial branches, ensures the rights and freedoms of its citizens. By comprehending how these branches function and interact, you gain insight into the mechanisms that safeguard democracy and freedom.

Equally important is understanding the rights and responsibilities that come with citizenship. From the privileges of voting and freedom of speech to the duties of jury service and community contribution, citizenship is a balance of benefits and obligations.

Knowledge of national symbols and landmarks, along with their historic significance, fosters a sense of pride and belonging. These symbols are not just emblematic of the nation's heritage but also of the collective memory and shared values of its people.

The path to citizenship also invites you to immerse yourself in the cultural diversity and societal values that define the American experience. This understanding promotes a deeper connection to the community and enriches the sense of identity.

Moreover, comprehending the basics of the U.S. economy, the role of taxes, and personal finance is crucial for navigating the practical aspects of life in the United States. This knowledge enables new citizens to make informed decisions and contribute economically to their new homeland.

Preparing for the USCIS Civics Test is a significant milestone on this journey. It requires not only memorization of facts but also an understanding of their relevance to American life and governance. Our guide aims to offer strategies, resources, and insights to ensure your success.

The final steps towards citizenship, including the citizenship interview and the Oath of Allegiance ceremony, are moments of great significance. They represent the culmination of your efforts and the beginning of a new chapter as a full participant in American democracy.

Life as a new U.S. citizen opens up avenues for continuous learning, civic involvement, and personal growth. Citizenship is not a static achievement but a starting point for engaging more deeply with the community and the nation.

In conclusion, embarking on the journey to U.S. citizenship is a transformative endeavor. It is a path paved with challenges and learning opportunities, but most importantly, it is a journey towards becoming part of a community that values freedom, respects diversity, and embraces civic responsibility. This guide is your companion in this journey, offering insights, encouragement, and comprehensive information to help you achieve the cherished goal of U.S. citizenship. Welcome to your journey.

CHAPTER 1:
THE AMERICAN DREAM BLUEPRINT: YOUR ULTIMATE GUIDE TO US CITIZENSHIP

The journey toward becoming a U.S. citizen is a transformative path that not only reshapes the life of an individual but also intertwines their story with the vast tapestry of America's history, cultures, and people. This journey, steeped in aspiration and achievement, is often referred to as pursuing the American Dream. It's a dream that promises freedom, opportunity, and a sense of belonging in a nation built by immigrants from every corner of the globe.

Embarking on this journey requires more than just the desire to call the United States your home. It asks for a commitment to understand the nation's values, history, and civics, which are foundational elements not only to pass the U.S. citizenship test but to thrive as a citizen. This chapter, and indeed this book, is crafted to be your companion through this significant phase of life. It's designed to navigate you through the nuances of U.S. history, government structure, civics, and society—equipping you with the knowledge needed to not only pass your citizenship test but to fully embrace the responsibilities and privileges that come with American citizenship.

The United States Citizenship and Immigration Services (USCIS) civics test is a vital step in your journey to citizenship. Unlike typical tests, this one is a doorway to an adopted homeland, a testament to your dedication and resilience. The test covers important topics on

U.S. history, the constitution, government structure, and more, emphasizing not just memorization, but an understanding of what it means to be an American.

To thrive in this journey, an immigrant doesn't simply absorb facts but engages with them, connecting personal narratives with the broader American story. It's a learning process that encompasses the sacrifices of the founders of this nation, the struggles and victories in its history, and the principles that uphold its democracy.

The blueprint for achieving the American Dream as laid out in this guide is comprehensive. It doesn't stop at preparing you for the civics test. It aims to integrate you into the fabric of American society, helping you understand your rights and responsibilities as a citizen, the importance of civic participation, and the values that Americans hold dear. It extends an invitation to not just live in the U.S. but to become a part of its ongoing story, contributing your own unique chapter.

Understanding the path to U.S. citizenship is the first crucial step. It involves not just knowing the eligibility criteria and the application process, but grasping the ethos of American citizenship. Whether you are navigating through naturalization, the green card gateway, or other visas leading to citizenship, each path has its own set of requirements and experiences that enrich your journey.

As we delve deeper into the heart of what it means to be an American, we explore the pivotal chapters of U.S. history, the underpinning principles of American democracy, and the structural complexities of its government. This foundational knowledge not only prepares you for the citizenship test but instills in you a sense of pride and belonging to a nation that cherishes liberty, equality, and the pursuit of happiness.

Civic participation and understanding your rights and responsibilities are another pillar of this journey. Voting, understanding the political system, contributing to the community, and staying informed are not just obligations but opportunities to shape the future of the country and ensure its democracy remains vibrant and inclusive.

The American society, with its diverse tapestry of cultures, traditions, and ideas, offers a rich backdrop for immigrants to weave their own stories into the nation's fabric. Understanding this diversity, and the values that unite Americans, is crucial for anyone looking to make the U.S. their home.

An insight into the U.S. economic landscape, including its market dynamics, the role of taxes, and personal finance, is also indispensable. It equips new citizens with the knowledge to succeed financially and understand their contributions to the economic vitality of the nation.

As we guide you through preparing for the USCIS civics test with effective study strategies and resources, we aim to build your confidence, ensuring you approach test day not just with memorized facts, but with a deep understanding and appreciation of what it means to be an American.

The journey doesn't end with passing the test or the naturalization ceremony. Becoming a U.S. citizen is merely the beginning of a lifelong engagement with the nation, its people, and its ideals. Continuous learning, staying informed, and active participation in civic life are what keeps the American Dream alive, ensuring it evolves and endures for generations to come.

This book, "The American Dream Blueprint: Your Ultimate Guide to US Citizenship," is more than a study guide; it's a roadmap to integrating into the heart and soul of the United States. It is your companion in understanding not only the rights but the shared responsibilities of citizenship. It seeks to inspire and motivate, to ignite a deep-seated sense of pride and belonging, and to prepare you fully for the significant step of becoming a U.S. citizen.

Embarking on this journey towards American citizenship is a bold step towards realizing personal dreams within the collective dream that is America. Here's to your courage, your hard work, and your unwavering spirit as you pursue your own chapter in the great American story.

Welcome to the path of understanding, engagement, and citizenship. Welcome to the journey of becoming an American.

CHAPTER 2:
UNDERSTANDING THE PATH TO US CITIZENSHIP

Navigating the journey towards U.S. citizenship can seem daunting, yet understanding the steps involved demystifies the process and sets a clear path forward. At its heart, the path to citizenship is a testament to one's commitment to fully embrace the rights and responsibilities that come with being a part of the American tapestry. As we delve into this crucial stage of your journey, we'll explore key aspects such as eligibility requirements, the application process, and the various paths that lead to becoming a citizen, including naturalization and the Green Card gateway. These routes are not just bureaucratic steps but milestones that mark your integration and acceptance into a nation that celebrates diversity, freedom, and democracy. Embrace this path with confidence and determination, for it leads to a world of opportunities and the chance to contribute to the great ongoing experiment that is America. Remember, each step taken on this path brings you closer not only to achieving personal goals but to becoming a vital part of a larger community committed to mutual respect, understanding, and shared prosperity.

Eligibility and Application Process

In your quest to turn the dream of US citizenship into reality, understanding the eligibility criteria and navigating the application process are pivotal first steps. Eligibility for citizenship through naturalization generally hinges on several key factors: you must be at least 18 years old, have been a permanent resident (a green card holder) for a specified period – usually five years, or three years if married to a US citizen, demonstrate continuous residence and physical presence in the United States, have the ability to read, write, and speak basic English, and show knowledge and understanding of U.S. history and government. Additionally, demonstrating good moral character and an attachment to the principles of the US Constitution is crucial. The application process begins with the Form N-400, the Application for Naturalization, followed by biometrics appointments, interviews, and finally, the civics and English tests.

The journey doesn't stop with knowing what to do; it's about embracing the path with dedication. Filling out your application is more than completing a form; it's a declaration of your intent to join the vibrant tapestry that is America. Yes, the road ahead involves paperwork, interviews, and tests – but each step is a milestone towards achieving the American Dream. Let this process be a testament to your resilience and commitment. The pride in passing the civics test, the joy of acing your interview, and the emotional depth of taking the Oath of Allegiance, all these experiences are threads in the larger fabric of the American narrative that you are about to join. Remember, becoming a US citizen is not just a change in legal status; it's an embrace of a shared history and a future filled with possibilities. Get set to contribute your unique thread to the American story.

Naturalization and the USCIS

Approaching the process of becoming a U.S. citizen through naturalization is a pivotal chapter in an individual's journey toward embracing the rights and responsibilities of American citizenship. The United States Citizenship and Immigration Services (USCIS) serves as the cornerstone of this transformative process, guiding applicants through the labyrinth of legal requirements and procedural steps necessary to achieve the American Dream.

Naturalization is more than just a legal process; it's a commitment to the American values of liberty, equality, and democracy. It involves understanding the history, government, and social fabric of the United States, a task that the USCIS supports through resources and learning materials designed to educate and inspire applicants.

To embark on this journey, one must first meet specific eligibility requirements set forth by the USCIS. These include, but are not limited to, being at least 18 years old, holding a Green Card (permanent residency) for a certain period, demonstrating continuous residence and physical presence in the United States, displaying an ability to read, write, and speak basic English, and having a basic understanding of U.S. history and government (civics).

Upon ensuring your eligibility, the next step is to complete Form N-400, the Application for Naturalization. This document is your initial introduction to the USCIS as a candidate for citizenship. Accuracy and honesty in completing this form are paramount, as any discrepancies can delay the process or lead to denial of the application.

After submitting your application, you will be scheduled for biometrics collection, where your fingerprints, photograph, and signature will be taken. This step is crucial for conducting a background check to ensure that all applicants meet the moral character requirement essential for U.S. citizenship.

One of the defining steps in the naturalization process is the civics test, where you'll demonstrate your knowledge of U.S. history and government. Preparation for this test is key, as it encompasses the principles upon which the United States was founded. The USCIS offers a variety of tools and resources to help you study and succeed.

An equally vital component of the naturalization process is the English language test, designed to assess your reading, writing, and speaking abilities. Mastery of the English language is seen not just as a requirement but as an essential tool for full participation in the economic, social, and political life of the American community.

Following the successful completion of these tests, you will be invited to attend an interview. This step allows USCIS officers to review your application, clarify any discrepancies, and evaluate your readiness to become a U.S. citizen. Approaching this interview with preparation and confidence is crucial.

The culmination of the naturalization process is the Oath of Allegiance Ceremony. Taking the Oath signifies a final and formal commitment to the United States and its Constitution, renouncing allegiance to any foreign sovereignty. As a participant, you're not just gaining citizenship; you're becoming an integral part of a diverse nation built on the ideals of freedom and opportunity for all.

Throughout the naturalization journey, the role of the USCIS is indispensable, not just in processing applications but in fostering an environment that supports immigrants' integration into the fabric of American society. Engaging with USCIS resources, attending naturalization workshops, and connecting with community organizations can provide valuable support and guidance.

Understanding the intricacies of the USCIS and the naturalization process can seem daunting at first glance. However, with each step, you are laying down the foundations for a new chapter in your life. This process is a testament to your resilience, determination, and commitment to embracing the values and responsibilities that come with American citizenship.

As you move forward, remember that naturalization is more than just obtaining a passport; it's an invitation to participate fully in the democratic life of the nation. Voting, volunteering, and engaging in community activities are just the beginning of the many ways you can contribute to the American story.

Let this journey to citizenship inspire you to strive for your personal and professional goals within the United States. The path to citizenship, guided by the USCIS, is your gateway to becoming an active participant in crafting the future of this nation. Naturalization is not just the end of an immigration process but the beginning of a lifetime of opportunities, rights, and responsibilities as a U.S. citizen.

In conclusion, approaching naturalization with dedication, preparation, and a profound respect for the principles that make the United States unique ensures not only the success of your application but the beginning of a rich, fulfilling experience as an American citizen. Embrace this journey with an open heart and mind, ready to contribute to and benefit from the collective tapestry that is America.

The Permanent Resident (Green Card) Gateway

Becoming a permanent resident or obtaining a green card is a monumental step on the journey toward U.S. citizenship. This pathway is filled with promise and opportunity, providing a stable foundation for those aspiring to fully embrace the American way of life.

At its core, the green card serves as proof of your lawful permanent resident status in the United States, offering you the freedom to live and work anywhere within the country. The journey to obtaining this status embodies the resilience and determination that are hallmarks of the immigrant experience.

One of the most critical aspects of the green card is that it sets the stage for naturalization, the process of becoming a U.S. citizen. After meeting certain residency and eligibility requirements, permanent residents can apply for citizenship, a move that opens the door to a myriad of benefits including the right to vote, protection from deportation, and eligibility for government jobs.

The path to securing a green card is varied, reflecting the diverse tapestry of individuals who seek to make the United States their home.

Whether through family connections, employment opportunities, refugee or asylum status, or other specialized categories, the journey is imbued with a sense of hope and aspiration for a new beginning.

For those navigating this path, it's crucial to understand the importance of maintaining your status with unwavering diligence. This includes abiding by the laws of the United States, supporting yourself financially, and ensuring you are not deemed removable under immigration law.

Moreover, the green card process is characterized by rigorous application procedures and screening processes. From background checks to interviews, each step is designed to ensure that applicants not only meet the eligibility criteria but are also well-suited to contribute positively to the fabric of American society.

It's worth noting that the journey doesn't end with obtaining a green card. Permanent residents must renew their status every ten years, a process that serves as a reminder of one's continuous commitment to their adopted country.

Furthermore, the green card gateway is not just about adhering to procedural and legal requirements. It's about embracing American values and principles. Learning about U.S. history, government, and civic responsibilities is integral to this process, enriching the immigrant's understanding of their new homeland and paving the way for meaningful participation in American democracy.

As permanent residents embark on this journey, they join a community of millions who have walked this path before them. This shared experience fosters a sense of belonging and identity within the broader mosaic of American culture.

The story of every immigrant is unique, yet the pursuit of the American dream unites them all. Holding a green card is more than just a legal status; it symbolizes hope, resilience, and the undying pursuit of opportunities. It is a testament to the enduring belief that anyone, regardless of where they come from, can make a significant contribution to society and lay down roots in the United States.

Embracing the path to U.S. citizenship through the green card gateway requires patience, perseverance, and preparation. It's a testament to one's determination to build a better life in the land of opportunity. This path is not without its challenges, but the rewards — freedom, security, and the chance to become an active participant in the American democratic process — are unparalleled.

Moreover, the influence of globalization and the interconnected nature of today's world underscore the importance of diversity and inclusion within the United States. Immigrants play a pivotal role in enriching the social, cultural, and economic fabric of the nation, bringing fresh perspectives, innovation, and vitality.

In essence, the green card is more than just a piece of plastic — it's a beacon of hope and a ticket to the American dream. It's an invitation to partake fully in the life of a nation built by immigrants, for immigrants. As such, pursuing U.S. citizenship through the permanent resident gateway is a noble endeavor, one that comes with responsibilities but also boundless possibilities.

So, as you take this step, remember that it's not just about the destination but also the journey. Cherish the experiences, learn from the challenges, and keep your eyes on the prize — becoming a U.S. citizen, with all the rights and responsibilities it entails. This is your pathway to making an indelible mark on the country that will become your home, contributing to its legacy of diversity, perseverance, and hope for future generations.

In conclusion, the green card gateway is a vital stepping stone on the path to U.S. citizenship. It symbolizes a commitment to the principles and ideals of the United States, offering a foundation upon which to build a new life and pursue the American dream. Aspiring citizens are encouraged to navigate this path with integrity, respect, and an open heart — traits that not only define the American spirit but also ensure success in this remarkable journey.

Other Paths: From Visas to Citizens

Embarking on the journey to U.S. citizenship can be both exhilarating and daunting. Beyond the well-trodden path of permanent residency or green cards, there exist alternative routes that pave the way for immigrants to achieve their American Dream. These paths may seem less straightforward, but they carry the promise of opening new doors to those seeking to call America their home.

One notable avenue is through various non-immigrant visas that may provide a stepping stone to permanent residency and, eventually, citizenship. For example, individuals who come to the U.S. on work visas such as the H-1B, which is designated for specialized occupations, may find opportunities to transition to a green card if sponsored by their employer. This path requires patience, as the process often involves years of waiting and meticulous paperwork, but the reward of embarking on the road to citizenship is undeniably worth the effort.

The U.S. is also home to a diversity lottery system, officially known as the Diversity Immigrant Visa program, which annually provides up to 50,000 visas to individuals from countries with low rates of immigration to the U.S. This program represents a unique path to obtaining a green card and, ultimately, citizenship. Applicants must meet simple but strict eligibility requirements, making it an enticing option for many around the globe.

Another critical path to consider is asylum or refugee status. Individuals who face persecution in their home countries because of their race, religion, nationality, membership in a particular social group, or political opinion may apply for asylum in the U.S. If granted, this provides a potential route to permanent residency after one year and is a stepping stone toward citizenship. This journey is fraught with challenges but stands as a beacon of hope for those in dire circumstances, demonstrating America's commitment to being a place of refuge.

For those with family ties in the U.S., family-based immigration presents a powerful path toward citizenship. U.S. citizens and lawful permanent residents can sponsor certain relatives for a green card. This pathway can sometimes be complex, requiring careful navigation of legal requirements and wait times. Yet, it underscores the importance of family reunification in the fabric of American immigration policy.

Investment is another avenue through which one might find their way to citizenship. The EB-5 visa program offers a green card to individuals who invest a significant amount in a U.S. business that creates or preserves at least ten full-time jobs for American workers. While this path demands considerable financial commitment, it offers a direct route to permanent residency for investors and their immediate family members.

It's essential to understand that each path to citizenship is accompanied by its set of challenges and rewards. Navigating the complex terrain of visas and immigration laws requires resilience, determination, and a deep understanding of the process. It's not just about meeting the requirements but also about embracing the spirit of what it means to be an American.

As immigrants embark on these diverse paths, they contribute to the rich tapestry of American society. Their journeys add to the story of a nation built on the strength of its people—people from all corners of the globe who choose to come together under the banner of freedom, opportunity, and unity.

The process of moving from a visa to citizenship can be lengthy and requires meticulous attention to detail. Keeping records, staying informed about changes in immigration policy, and seeking guidance from experts are all critical steps in ensuring a successful transition.

Moreover, integration into American society is a pivotal part of the journey toward citizenship. Learning English, understanding U.S. civics, and engaging with the community are not just requirements for naturalization; they are ways to forge a deeper connection with one's adopted country and lay the groundwork for a successful future here.

Throughout this process, it's vital to remain motivated and inspired. The road to U.S. citizenship is paved with stories of perseverance, hard work, and the unyielding belief in the pursuit of a better life. These stories are a testament to the enduring spirit of those who choose to embark on this journey, reinforcing the belief that citizenship is more than a legal status—it's a symbol of one's dedication to becoming a part of the American fabric.

In conclusion, while the journey from visas to citizenship may differ from one individual to another, the destination remains the same: a chance to participate fully in the life of the United States. With commitment, the journey can lead to not just a new nationality but an opportunity to contribute to the ongoing story of a nation continually enriched by its diversity. As immigrants navigate these paths, they don't just seek to change their status; they aim to change their lives and, in turn, enrich the American experience for all.

The paths from visas to citizenship, with all their intricacies and challenges, embody the dynamism at the heart of the American immigration narrative. By understanding and navigating these routes, individuals take essential steps toward realizing their dreams and affirming the values that have long made America a beacon of hope for people around the world.

CHAPTER 3:
THE HISTORY OF THE UNITED STATES

Embarking on the journey through the history of the United States is akin to unfolding a map that guides us not only to understand the present but also to navigate our future. This grand narrative begins before the ink dried on the Declaration of Independence, tracing back to the early settlements, through the courageous battles for autonomy, and onward to a country's relentless pursuit of growth and equality. It is a tale of resilience, where from the ashes of conflict a nation emerged, dedicated to the ideals of liberty and justice for all. As you gear up to call this spirited land your home, it's crucial to grasp the intricate tapestry of events and ideologies that have shaped its course. This understanding not only prepares you for the USCIS civics test but also enriches your appreciation for the profound journey of transformation this country has undergone. From the first settlers' quest for religious freedom to the Founding Fathers' vision of a sovereign nation, the narrative of the United States is a testament to the power of unity amidst diversity. As you delve into this chapter, let it inspire you with the courage of those who came before, inviting you to contribute your thread to the ever-evolving American story, where your dreams, too, find a place in its vast, inclusive horizon.

The Founding Pillars

Embarking on the voyage to understand the bustling, diverse, and ever-evolving narrative of the United States, we land upon the critical foundation known as the Founding Pillars. These pillars don't just hold up a physical structure; they represent the core ideals, principles, and values that have shaped the nation from its inception to its current status as a global beacon of democracy, liberty, and opportunity. For anyone preparing to make the United States their new home, grasping these concepts isn't just part of a test; it's understanding the heart of what it means to be an American.

The journey of the United States is one of unparalleled courage, innovation, and unyielding pursuit of freedom. The story begins with the groundwork laid by the Declaration of Independence in 1776, a document proclaiming the colonies' determination to create a sovereign nation free from British rule. This daring declaration is the first pillar, fostering a new era where life, liberty, and the pursuit of happiness became unalienable rights, guiding the nation's ethos.

The second pillar is the Constitution, a living document crafted in 1787, that outlines the framework of the government and safeguards the liberties of its citizens through a system of checks and balances. This ingenious structure ensures no single branch gains too much power, a testament to the founders' vision for a nation where freedom and justice reign supreme.

Bolstering the Constitution, the third pillar is the Bill of Rights, the first ten amendments that explicitly guarantee individual freedoms like speech, assembly, and religion. These rights are the bedrock upon which American society stands, ensuring that every citizen's liberties are protected, making the United States a sanctuary for those who yearn for freedom and opportunity.

But the Founding Pillars go beyond documents and amendments. They embody the spirit of resilience and determination, as seen in the collective will of the people. This unity and drive are the fourth pillar, an unseen yet palpable force that has steered the country through trials and triumphs, from civil war and economic depressions to monumental civil rights movements and technological breakthroughs.

Furthermore, the melting pot of cultures, religions, and backgrounds that make up the fabric of American society is the fifth pillar. This diversity is not just a characteristic of the nation; it's a source of strength, innovation, and global leadership. Embracing this melting pot means recognizing that every citizen, no matter their origin, contributes to the tapestry of the nation.

Education and the relentless pursuit of knowledge form the sixth pillar. The United States, home to some of the world's leading universities and think tanks, places a high value on education as a means of empowerment, socio-economic mobility, and civic engagement. Through education, individuals garner the tools needed to contribute meaningfully to society and the global community.

The entrepreneurial spirit that runs deep in American history is the seventh pillar. From the industrial revolution to the technological boom, this spirit has propelled the nation forward, fostering growth, job creation, and global competitiveness. This relentless drive for innovation reflects the nation's adaptable and forward-thinking mindset.

An adherence to the rule of law forms the eighth pillar, essential for maintaining order, protecting rights, and ensuring justice. The United States' commitment to the rule of law stands as a pillar of its democracy, providing a framework within which freedom can flourish.

The ninth pillar is the commitment to civic engagement and community service. The United States thrives because of its active citizens who volunteer, vote, engage in public discourse, and serve in various capacities to improve their communities. This engagement embodies the essence of democracy and the responsibilities that come with the freedoms enjoyed.

Last but not least, the tenth pillar is the relentless pursuit of a more perfect union. Recognizing that the work of democracy is never complete, this pillar embodies the spirit of continuous improvement, striving for social justice, equality, and an unwavering commitment to live up to the ideals upon which the nation was founded.

Each of these pillars supports not just the structure of a nation, but the dynamic and ever-evolving dream that is America. They are a testament to the fact that while the country has faced and continues to face challenges, its foundation is strong, allowing for growth, change, and the continued pursuit of a better future for all its citizens.

Understanding these pillars is essential for anyone looking to make their home in the United States. They provide a blueprint for what it means to be American, highlighting the values, rights, and responsibilities that come with citizenship. They inspire us to contribute positively to our communities, to cherish and protect our freedoms, and to continually strive towards the ideals that these pillars represent.

As you prepare for the citizenship test and, more importantly, for your life as an American citizen, take these pillars to heart. Let them guide you in your journey, inspire you to engage with your new home, and remind you of the enduring principles upon which the United States was built. Welcome to a nation of dreamers, doers, and believers in a better tomorrow.

From Colonization to Independence

The journey from the first European settlements on what would become US soil to the birth of a nation independent of British rule is both complex and fascinating. It's a story of ambition, struggle, and the relentless pursuit of freedom. Understanding this history is crucial for anyone looking to become a part of the American fabric through citizenship.

The story begins in the early 17th century when Europeans began establishing permanent settlements. The Jamestown Colony, founded in 1607 by the English, was among the first successful settlements.

These early settlers faced immense challenges, from harsh winters to conflicts with Native American tribes. Yet, their determination laid the groundwork for future colonies.

By the mid-17th century, the Thirteen Colonies were established along the Atlantic coast. Each colony had its own government and operated with a degree of autonomy from the British crown. This period saw a diverse influx of people seeking various freedoms and opportunities. The concept of religious freedom, in particular, was a significant motivator for settlers, leading to the establishment of colonies like Massachusetts by the Pilgrims in 1620.

The relationship between the colonies and Britain began to deteriorate in the mid-18th century. The British government imposed a series of taxes and regulations designed to exert greater control over the colonies, such as the Stamp Act of 1765 and the Tea Act of 1773. Colonists viewed these acts as unjust, sparking a series of protests and events, like the Boston Tea Party in 1773, that would lead to the Revolutionary War.

The call for independence grew stronger, and in 1776, leaders from each of the Thirteen Colonies gathered to sign the Declaration of Independence. This document, primarily authored by Thomas Jefferson, articulated the colonies' reasons for seeking independence and established the fundamental principles that would guide the new nation.

The Revolutionary War, lasting from 1775 to 1783, was a tumultuous period. The colonies faced a well-equipped British military with a network of supporters who believed in the cause of independence. The war was not just fought on the battlefields; it was also a war of ideas. The notion that people have the right to govern themselves was revolutionary.

The American victory at Saratoga in 1777 was a turning point in the war, convincing France to enter the conflict on the side of the colonies. This alliance was pivotal, providing the Americans with additional military support and resources.

The war concluded with the signing of the Treaty of Paris in 1783, which recognized the independence of the United States. The aftermath of the war was not without challenges, as the young nation struggled to find its footing. The Articles of Confederation, initially drafted as the nation's first constitution, proved to be too weak to handle the country's needs.

The Constitutional Convention of 1787 was a turning point, leading to the drafting of the US Constitution. This document established a federal government with a system of checks and balances, a revolutionary idea that ensured no single branch could wield unchecked power. The Constitution was designed to protect the liberties fought for in the Revolutionary War while providing a robust framework for governance.

The United States of America, as it emerged from the Constitutional Convention, was a nation founded on ideals of liberty, democracy, and the pursuit of happiness. These were not just abstract concepts; they were principles that guided the fledgling nation as it navigated the challenges of governance, expansion, and internal conflict.

The journey to independence was marked by a collective realization that freedom was not only worth fighting for but also required a commitment to building a system of government that reflected the values and aspirations of its citizens. The Constitution's ratification and the subsequent Bill of Rights were milestones in this journey, reflecting a commitment to individual rights and liberties.

As immigrants and students of American history, understanding this period offers valuable insights into the country's foundational principles. It serves as a reminder of the resilience and determination of those who fought to establish a nation where freedom and democracy were paramount.

The story of America's journey from colonization to independence is a testament to the power of collective action and the enduring relevance of the ideals upon which the United States was founded. It exemplifies the possibility of change and the importance of striving for a better, more inclusive society.

In preparing for the US citizenship test, reflecting on this history can provide both inspiration and a deeper appreciation for the rights and responsibilities that come with American citizenship. It's not just about memorizing facts; it's about understanding the sacrifices made and the vision pursued to establish a country where the rule of law, individual liberties, and the pursuit of happiness prevail.

As you continue your journey to becoming a part of this great nation, let the lessons of history inspire you to contribute positively to its future, uphold its ideals, and take active participation in its democratic processes. The story of America's independence is a reminder of what can be achieved when people unite for a common cause and demand a fair and just society.

Expansion and Conflict: A Growing Nation

The journey of the United States, characterized by both remarkable expansion and intense conflict, embodies a pivotal chapter in the nation's history. As we delve into this era, we're not just tracing the geographical growth of a country, but also exploring the dynamics of a society grappling with its identity, challenges, and aspirations. This story mirrors the essence of human persistence and the unyielding quest for progress, resonating deeply with those aiming to call this land their home.

In the wake of gaining independence, the young nation found itself teetering on the edge of a vast, uncharted continent that promised untold opportunities. Driven by the concept of Manifest Destiny, the belief that the expansion of the US across the American continents was both justified and inevitable, settlers pushed westward. This era was marked by a formidable expansion that doubled the nation's size and sketched the outline of its modern geography.

However, this growth was not without its conflicts. As the nation expanded, it encountered a complex web of disputes that tested its resolve. The acquisition of territories such as Louisiana, Texas, and beyond sparked debates over slavery, sovereignty, and the very shape of the nation's future. The Mexican-American War and the controversial annexation of Texas underscored the contentious nature of American expansion.

Amidst these external expansions, the internal struggle over slavery intensified. The Missouri Compromise and the Kansas-Nebraska Act attempted to balance the scales between free and slave states, yet only served to deepen the divide. This period underscored the complexity of navigating economic interests, moral values, and regional identities within a growing nation.

The Dred Scott decision, denying citizenship to African American slaves, further polarized the nation. This controversial ruling not only illuminated the entrenched system of slavery but also questioned the foundation of American liberty and justice. For immigrants striving to understand the ethos of the United States, this chapter reveals the complexities of its democratic principles in the face of profound moral challenges.

The relentless push for expansion also brought the United States into bitter conflict with Native American tribes. The Trail of Tears is a stark reminder of the heavy cost paid by the indigenous people for American progress. This tragic event highlights the darker facets of expansion and poses sobering questions about justice and human rights in the march toward national growth.

The culmination of these tensions led to the Civil War, a defining conflict that threatened to tear the nation apart. The war was not just a battle over territory, but a profound struggle over the values that would define America. It tested the resilience of the Union and the principle that all men are created equal, eventually leading to the abolition of slavery with the 13th amendment.

Reconstruction followed, aiming to rebuild a shattered nation and integrate freed slaves into the fabric of American life. However, the promises of Reconstruction were unevenly realized, illustrating the ongoing challenge of living up to the ideals of liberty and equality. This period was a critical test of America's commitment to its founding principles and to forging a more inclusive society.

As we reflect on this era of expansion and conflict, we see a tableau of human endeavor, resilience, and aspiration. It's a narrative that underscores the importance of understanding history, not just as a chronicle of bygone events, but as a guide to navigating the present and shaping the future. For those seeking to be part of this nation, these stories offer both caution and inspiration.

Engaging with this chapter of American history empowers us to appreciate the complexity and the richness of the nation's journey. It highlights the significance of unity, the value of diverse perspectives, and the unending quest for a more perfect union. As immigrants and future citizens, embracing these lessons can inspire us to contribute to the ongoing American narrative, ensuring that the dream of democracy, liberty, and opportunity remains vibrant and inclusive for all.

In this light, the story of American expansion and conflict is not just a testament to what has been overcome but also a beacon for what can be achieved. It champions the spirit of perseverance, the importance of justice, and the indispensable value of empathy and understanding in the quest for common ground. These are the principles that fortify the American spirit and guide its progress. They are the same values that greet newcomers with the promise of a new beginning, inviting them to partake in the continuous endeavor to achieve the American dream.

For immigrants, understanding this phase of American history is pivotal. It offers a lens through which to view the present, understanding the layers and complexities of American society today. Recognizing the struggles and triumphs of the past can help forge a sense of belonging and ownership over the shared future.

As we turn our gaze towards the horizon, the journey of expansion and conflict in the United States serves as a reminder of the power of collective effort in the face of daunting challenges. It reinforces the idea that amidst adversity lies the opportunity for growth, improvement, and unity. For those on the path to citizenship, this story is not merely historical—it's a source of inspiration and courage on the journey to becoming an integral part of this great nation.

In concluding, the era of expansion and conflict encapsulates a critical chapter in the American saga—one of resilience through adversity, of progress amidst division, and of a nation continually striving to fulfill its promise. For immigrants and future citizens, it represents a profound narrative of transformation and hope, embodying the enduring spirit of the United States. By learning from this rich history, we can all contribute to the ongoing story of America, building a legacy of unity, justice, and opportunity for generations to come.

CHAPTER 4:
PRINCIPLES OF AMERICAN
DEMOCRACY

In the tapestry of American society, understanding the principles of American democracy is akin to grasping the very threads that make up the fabric of the nation itself. It's a system built on the bedrock of values such as liberty, equality, and the pursuit of happiness, encapsulated within the Constitution and the Bill of Rights. These documents don't just serve as historical artifacts; they're living affirmations of the rights and freedoms every citizen is entitled to. As we delve into the nuances of federalism, it becomes clear how this ingenious system of shared power between states and the federal government ensures that democracy is both resilient and adaptable. The rule of law and the role of the courts are equally pivotal, safeguarding the rights of individuals against the excesses of power. This intricate dance of checks and balances, rights and responsibilities, is not just theoretical. It's a call to action for every person who calls America home, whether by birth or choice, to partake actively in this ongoing democratic experiment. Understanding these principles is not just about preparing for the citizenship test; it's about embedding oneself in the rich tapestry of America's democratic tradition, and nurturing it forward for generations to come.

The Constitution and the Bill of Rights

The Constitution of the United States is not just a piece of paper; it's the very backbone of American democracy. Created in 1787, it established a federal government, setting out the rules and principles that govern the country. Think of the Constitution as the blueprint for America's democratic experiment, one that has been remarkably enduring and adaptable.

At its heart, the Constitution organizes the government into three branches: the Legislative, the Executive, and the Judicial. This separation of powers ensures that no single entity holds too much control, creating a balance that sustains democracy. Each branch has its role, its power, and its means of balancing the others. It's an intricate dance of checks and balances designed to safeguard liberty and prevent tyranny.

However, the story doesn't end with the original seven articles of the Constitution. The Bill of Rights, the first ten amendments added in 1791, is equally fundamental. These amendments guarantee individual freedoms and rights, including freedom of speech, the press, and religion; the right to bear arms; and the rights to fair legal proceedings. By including the Bill of Rights, the framers addressed the concerns of those wary of a too-powerful central government, ensuring protections for individual liberties.

One of the most beautiful aspects of the Constitution is its ability to adapt over time through amendments. Amending the Constitution is intentionally challenging, requiring significant consensus across the political spectrum. This process ensures that changes reflect a broad agreement rather than fleeting popular opinion. To date, there have been 27 amendments, including those that abolished slavery, granted women the right to vote, and defined citizenship.

The Constitution and the Bill of Rights reflect a deep understanding of human nature and governance. They establish a legal and ethical framework that guides the United States. It's a system designed not only to govern but to protect the governed. It recognizes the potential for government to overreach while also emphasizing the individual's role in democratic governance.

For immigrants and those pursuing US citizenship, understanding the Constitution and the Bill of Rights is crucial. It's not just about passing a test; it's about grasping the principles that shape American life. This understanding fosters a deeper connection to the country and its values, laying a solid foundation for meaningful participation in its democracy.

Learning about the Constitution reveals the evolving nature of American democracy. Amendments like the 15th, 19th, and 26th, which expanded voting rights, show the nation's progress toward a more inclusive democracy. They highlight the role of activism and advocacy in driving change, showing that the Constitution is a living document, responsive to the growth and change of the society it governs.

The Constitution's preamble itself sets an inspirational goal: "to form a more perfect Union." It acknowledges the country's ongoing journey towards improvement and refinement. This journey is collective, involving every citizen's engagement and participation. It's a call to action, inviting every individual to contribute to the nation's progress, safeguarding its democracy and freedoms.

The Bill of Rights serves as a constant reminder of the individual freedoms guaranteed to all citizens. These rights are not just legal technicalities; they're the pillars of American life. Understanding these rights is vital for all, especially for immigrants integrating into American society. It empowers them, enabling effective engagement with the community and the government.

Significantly, the Constitution and the Bill of Rights also delineate limits. They establish boundaries for government action, protecting individuals from unjust treatment. This balance between enabling government power and restraining it is delicate and essential. It's a balance that ensures the government serves the people, not the other way around.

For future citizens, the journey through American democracy is not just about acquiring rights but also embracing responsibilities. The Constitution establishes the framework for participation in democracy, encouraging an informed and active citizenry. It's a call to be engaged, to vote, to serve on juries, and to participate in the democratic process.

The Constitution and the Bill of Rights embody the American ideal of liberty and justice for all. They are living documents, reflective of the nation's struggles and achievements in its pursuit of these ideals. They invite every citizen, whether by birth or by choice, to play an active role in this ongoing pursuit.

Your journey to US citizenship offers a unique opportunity to connect with these foundational principles. It's a chance to understand the roots of American democracy and to affirm your commitment to its ideals. The Constitution isn't just a historical document—it's a roadmap for active, engaged citizenship.

As you prepare for your citizenship test, remember that you're not just studying facts. You're embracing a legacy of democracy, rights, and responsibilities. You're joining a community committed to a set of shared values, expressed through the Constitution and the Bill of Rights. It's a powerful step toward becoming not just a citizen, but a guardian of American democracy.

In conclusion, the Constitution and the Bill of Rights are more than just sections on a citizenship test; they are embodiments of American democracy. They symbolize the nation's commitment to freedom, equality, and the rule of law. By understanding these documents, you're not just preparing for a test; you're preparing to be an active participant in one of the world's oldest ongoing experiments in self-governance. Welcome to the journey.

Federalism: The States and the Federal Government

Federalism in the United States is a cornerstone of how the country operates, blending power between the national government and the states in a way that empowers regions while maintaining a unified national policy. Understanding this principle is not only crucial for digesting the American political landscape but also inspiring for those aspiring to become U.S. citizens. It's a testament to the balance of autonomy and collaboration.

The genesis of federalism in the United States can be traced back to the Founding Fathers, who, after experiencing the limitations of the Articles of Confederation, sought a system that could unite the states under a strong national government without stripping them of their powers. This delicate balance was intended to prevent tyranny, promote democracy, and allow for local governance to address regional concerns effectively.

At its core, federalism is about dividing powers between the federal government and the states. The U.S. Constitution outlines this division, granting certain powers exclusively to the national government, such as the ability to regulate interstate commerce, declare war, and establish post offices. Conversely, powers not explicitly reserved for the federal government are considered the domain of state governments. This includes areas like education, local law enforcement, and intrastate transportation.

One of the most striking features of federalism is that it allows states to act as "laboratories of democracy". States have the freedom to experiment with policies and solutions that reflect the diverse needs and values of their citizens. This aspect of federalism encourages innovation and allows for a diversity of approaches to solving common problems.

However, federalism also means navigating a complex relationship between state and federal laws. At times, conflicts arise when there's a question of which level of government has the authority over a particular area. The Supremacy Clause of the Constitution establishes that federal law takes precedence over state law when there's a conflict, ensuring a unified legal framework.

The relationship between the states and the federal government is not static; it evolves in response to changing political, social, and economic conditions. Over the years, various legal decisions, amendments to the Constitution, and legislation have reshaped federalism, adjusting the balance of power to meet the needs of the time.

An essential aspect of federalism is the protection of individual liberties. By dispersing power, federalism helps to prevent any one entity from gaining too much control, thus protecting freedom and democracy. This principle is deeply ingrained in the American political system and speaks to the ongoing effort to balance governmental authority with individual rights.

For immigrants and those on the path to citizenship, understanding federalism is more than an academic exercise; it's about grasping the fundamental principles that shape life in the United States. It highlights the importance of engaging at both the state and national levels, recognizing how both spheres of government impact daily life.

The mechanics of federalism also underscore the value of civic participation. Voting in both state and federal elections, getting involved in community issues, and understanding the nuances of local versus national governance are all critical for those who seek to fully embrace their role as citizens.

Moreover, federalism reinforces the concept of unity in diversity. It allows for a multitude of voices to be heard and represented in the political process, celebrating the diversity that immigrants bring to the

American tapestry. This dynamic shapes a society that is resilient, adaptable, and inclusive.

In studying for the USCIS Civics Test, a deep dive into federalism provides not just knowledge but a blueprint for active citizenship. It prepares future citizens to engage thoughtfully with their new country, appreciating the complexities and opportunities of its governance system.

While federalism can sometimes lead to tensions between state and federal governments, these disputes are part of a lively dialogue about democracy, power, and governance. They reflect a system that is always striving to find the right balance, ensuring that both unity and diversity can thrive.

The journey to U.S. citizenship is not just a legal process but an invitation to join a community of shared values and principles. Federalism, with its emphasis on balance, collaboration, and respect for diversity, embodies the spirit of the American political experiment. It's a testament to the belief that a multitude of voices, working together, can create a stronger, more vibrant democracy.

As you prepare for the citizenship test and reflect on what it means to be an American, remember that federalism is a symbol of the country's enduring commitment to democratic ideals. It stands as a powerful reminder of America's promise: a nation that values the contributions of all its citizens, fosters innovation, and guards against the concentration of power, ensuring liberty and justice for all.

In conclusion, federalism is not just a section on a test but a living, breathing principle that animates the American government and its citizens. It's a principle that calls for your participation, your voice, and your commitment to the ideals of democracy. Embrace it as you step into the role of a U.S. citizen, ready to contribute to the country's ongoing story of unity, diversity, and democratic governance.

The Rule of Law and the Role of the Courts

The bedrock of American democracy is the rule of law, a principle that everyone, from the most influential leaders to ordinary citizens, is subject to the same laws. This universal principle ensures fairness, equity, and justice within the society, forming the foundation upon which trust in government and societal institutions is built. It's a concept that might seem straightforward, yet its execution and maintenance are anything but simple. They require the unwavering commitment of the judiciary, legislative, and executive branches of government to uphold these laws consistently and fairly.

At the heart of this system is the role of the courts, which interpret and apply the law in real world scenarios. Courts are tasked with a critical balancing act; they must protect the rights of individuals while also ensuring that societal order is maintained. This role can often place them at the center of hotly debated issues, reflecting the evolving nature of societal values and norms. Understanding the function of courts within the rule of law offers insight into the complex, dynamic machinery of American democracy.

In America, courts operate at both the federal and state levels, allowing for a broad and nuanced interpretation of laws that reflects the diverse values and needs of its people. This dual system ensures that justice is administered in a manner that is both accessible and responsive to the local community, while also consistent with overarching constitutional principles. It's a unique feature of the American legal system that underscores the importance of balance between centralized authority and local autonomy.

One might wonder, what makes the rule of law so vital to democracy? It's simple yet profound: the rule of law prevents the arbitrary use of power. Without it, the rights and freedoms that form the essence of democracy could easily be undermined by those in positions of authority. The courts serve as the guardians of these rights, interpreting the constitution and other laws to ensure that government actions do not overstep their bounds. This protective role of the judiciary is a key component of the checks and balances system that is fundamental to American government.

It's also important to recognize how the rule of law fosters a culture of accountability. Public officials, from local council members to the President, are held accountable under the same legal standards as private citizens. This accountability is enforced through the courts, which have the authority to judge the legality of official actions and impose penalties on those who violate the law. This ensures that power is not only checked but balanced in a way that protects the rights and interests of all citizens.

Moreover, the rule of law and the role of courts contribute to a stable and predictable legal environment, encouraging economic growth and social progress. Businesses can operate with confidence, knowing that contracts will be enforced and property rights respected. Similarly, individuals are more likely to engage in civic life and pursue their interests when they believe that fair treatment will be accorded to them under the law. This predictability and stability are essential for fostering an environment where freedom, innovation, and prosperity can flourish.

However, maintaining the rule of law is not without its challenges. Courts must navigate complex legal and moral questions, often in the face of public scrutiny and political pressure. Judges and justices, the individuals who make up these courts, are humans who bring their perspectives and understanding to the bench. Yet, their commitment to impartiality, to deciding cases based on evidence and legal principles, rather than personal belief or political expediency, is what maintains public confidence in the judicial system.

It's a testament to the strength of the American judicial system that, despite these challenges, the courts have consistently acted as a bulwark against tyranny and oppression. The landmark decisions in cases like Brown v. Board of Education and Marbury v. Madison illustrate the courts' role in advancing civil rights and ensuring governmental power is not misused.

Engagement with the legal system is another aspect where citizens play a vital role. Jury service, for instance, offers a direct way for individuals to participate in the judicial process, upholding the principle that justice is not the domain of a select few but a community responsibility. Through such participation, citizens contribute to the legitimacy and effectiveness of the rule of law, reinforcing the foundation of American democracy.

Furthermore, the legal system in the United States is dynamic, constantly evolving to address new challenges and societal shifts. Courts interpret laws in a contemporary context, demonstrating the adaptability and resilience of the American judiciary. This evolving nature underscores the significance of continuous learning and engagement with the legal system for every citizen.

For immigrants seeking to become citizens, understanding the rule of law and the role of courts is not just about passing a test; it's about grasping the essence of what it means to be part of a democratic society. It's a realization that their rights and freedoms are protected, that they too have a role in upholding the principles of justice and equality that define America.

This chapter has laid out the significance of the rule of law and the role of the courts as foundational elements of American democracy. As you continue on your journey to citizenship, remember that your participation in this system, your understanding and respect for the law, contribute to the strength and vitality of the nation. It's a responsibility that holds great challenges but offers even greater rewards: the promise of a fair, just, and free society.

Reflecting on the principles discussed here will not only prepare you for the USCIS civics test but will also equip you with a deeper appreciation for the values that underpin American life. As you move forward, embrace the opportunities and responsibilities that come with being part of a democratic society. Engage with your community, stay informed, and exercise your rights with the understanding that in doing so, you help perpetuate the rule of law and the very essence of democracy itself.

CHAPTER 5:
THE AMERICAN GOVERNMENT
STRUCTURE

The backbone of American democracy is its distinct structure of government, a blueprint for freedom and governance that has withstood the test of time. This chapter delves into the intricacies of the American government's structure, designed to balance power through the separation of powers across three branches: the Executive, Legislative, and Judicial. The Executive Branch, led by the President, embodies the nation's leadership and enforces laws. Meanwhile, the Legislative Branch, or Congress, consisting of the House of Representatives and the Senate, crafts the nation's laws with a pulse on the diverse voices of the American people. The Judicial Branch, with the Supreme Court at its helm, ensures the laws adhere to the Constitution's principles. Understanding this tripartite system is not just an academic exercise; it's about seeing how these branches work seamlessly to build a government that is of the people, by the people, for the people. Embracing this knowledge empowers one to navigate the rights and responsibilities of citizenship with confidence and pride, laying the groundwork for not just passing the USCIS civics test but becoming an engaged and informed citizen. This system, with its checks and balances, is designed to prevent any one branch from gaining too much power, ensuring liberty and justice remain the cornerstones of American democracy.

The Executive Branch: Powers and Responsibilities

The heart of any vibrant democracy is its ability to change, adapt, and grow. The United States, with its complex yet profoundly effective system of governance, provides a prime example of this dynamism. Central to this system is the Executive Branch, a body vested with significant powers and responsibilities, designed to ensure not just the enforcement of laws but the very functioning of democracy itself.

At the helm of the Executive Branch sits the President of the United States, a leader elected every four years through a process that embodies the nation's commitment to democracy. The president's primary role is to execute and enforce federal laws, made possible through the powers vested in them by the Constitution. This responsibility is a cornerstone of the American government structure, impacting citizens' lives domestically and shaping the nation's relationships abroad.

Among the key powers of the presidency is the ability to sign legislation into law or to veto bills passed by Congress, illustrating the system of checks and balances that is fundamental to American democracy. This power acts as a safeguard against the passage of laws that may not serve the nation's best interest, ensuring that every piece of legislation is carefully considered by both the Legislative and the Executive branches.

The president also serves as the Commander-in-Chief of the Armed Forces, highlighting the profound trust and responsibility placed in this office. This role encompasses not only the defense of the United States but also the responsibility to make critical decisions that can impact global peace and security. It's a sobering reminder of the weight of duty that comes with the office.

In addition to these responsibilities, the President has the authority to appoint federal officials, including judges to the Supreme Court, subject to Senate confirmation. This power extends the president's influence over the federal judiciary, underscoring the interconnected nature of the American government's branches.

The Executive Branch is also tasked with conducting foreign affairs. Through the negotiation of treaties, the appointment of ambassadors, and the overall direction of American foreign policy, the president plays a pivotal role in defining the United States' stance on the global stage. This aspect of the presidency highlights the intricate balance between domestic policies and international relations.

Moreover, the president holds the responsibility to ensure the federal government's smooth operation, including the execution of the budget and the oversight of executive departments and agencies. This task requires a keen understanding of the nation's needs and a thorough administration of the vast machinery of government.

The Vice President, while often viewed in the context of their role as the President's successor, also serves as the President of the Senate, casting the tie-breaking vote in the Senate when necessary. This role exemplifies the Vice President's importance in the legislative process, ensuring smooth operations within the federal government.

Executive Orders represent another critical tool at the President's disposal, allowing them to manage the operations of the federal government directly. Through these orders, the president can enact significant changes and policies, further illustrating the executive power's breadth and depth.

Beyond these formal powers, the President also has a duty to inspire and lead the nation, acting as a symbol of American values and democracy. This less tangible aspect of the presidency is crucial for maintaining national unity and guiding the country through times of trouble and triumph alike.

It's important to recognize that the Executive Branch does not operate in isolation. Its powers and responsibilities are checked by the other branches of government to prevent any misuse of power. This system of checks and balances is what ensures that no single branch becomes too powerful, maintaining the democratic principles upon which the United States was founded.

The role of the Executive Branch in American government is thus multifaceted and profound. It encompasses a range of duties from the enforcement of laws to the leadership of the nation on the global stage. For those preparing for the USCIS civics test, understanding the powers and responsibilities of the Executive Branch is not just about memorizing facts. It's about appreciating the complexities and the nuances of American governance, an understanding that will deepen your connection to your future homeland.

As you continue on your journey to becoming a US citizen, remember that the fabric of this nation is woven from the contributions of individuals from all walks of life. Your journey, aspirations, and dreams contribute to this rich tapestry. The understanding of the Executive Branch, its powers, and its responsibilities, is more than academic knowledge—it's a step towards fully embracing the rights and duties of citizenship.

The Executive Branch, with its blend of power and accountability, mirrors the American ethos of leadership with responsibility. It offers a unique insight into the governance model that has steered the United States through centuries of change and challenges. As you prepare to become a part of this continuous story, know that understanding the roles and duties within the American government is a foundational step toward active and informed citizenship.

In the end, the role of the Executive Branch reminds us that governance is not just about power but about service and leadership. It's a lesson in the responsibility that comes with authority, the need for vision combined with integrity, and the crucial balance between strength and accountability. Embrace this knowledge, for it embodies the principles of democracy and the promise of the American Dream.

The Legislative Branch: Congress in Action

Embarking on the journey to understand the American government, particularly its legislative branch, is crucial for grasping how policies and laws that affect the daily lives of citizens and immigrants alike are made. Congress, the heart of the legislative branch, embodies democracy in action, representing the voices of the American people from every corner of the nation. Its proceedings and decisions shape the path of the United States in significant ways.

At its core, Congress is bicameral, consisting of two chambers: the Senate and the House of Representatives. This structure, a result of the Great Compromise during the Constitutional Convention in 1787, ensures a balance of power, offering equal representation in the Senate while basing representation in the House on population. Such a design reflects the founders' intent to accommodate both the small and large states, creating a framework for collaboration and debate that lies at the heart of American democracy.

The Senate, often referred to as the "upper house," is composed of 100 senators, with each state represented by two senators, regardless of its size or population. This ensures that even the smallest states have a strong voice in the legislative process. Senators serve six-year terms, with approximately one-third of the Senate being elected every two years. This continuity and staggered election cycle lend the Senate a sense of stability and deep experience within its ranks.

The House of Representatives, known as the "lower house," currently has 435 members who represent congressional districts. These districts are apportioned based on population, as determined by the decennial census. Representatives serve two-year terms, making the House more immediately responsive to changes in public sentiment.

The House's structure facilitates a closer connection to the electorate, ensuring that the diverse voices and concerns of the American people are heard in Congress.

One of Congress's fundamental roles is the drafting, debating, and passing of legislation. This process is intricate and designed to ensure thorough consideration. A bill, or proposed law, can originate in either chamber (except for revenue bills, which must start in the House). Once a bill is introduced, it is assigned to a committee for detailed evaluation. Committees play a crucial role, scrutinizing the bill's content, holding hearings, and often making amendments before the bill is debated by the full chamber.

If a bill passes one chamber, it proceeds to the other for consideration. Should the second chamber approve the bill, often after further amendment and debate, it is sent to the President. The President then has the option to sign the bill into law or veto it. Congress can override a presidential veto with a two-thirds majority vote in both chambers, a testament to the system's checks and balances designed to prevent the concentration of too much power in any single branch of government.

In addition to its legislative responsibilities, Congress plays a vital role in the federal budget process. This includes assessing and authorizing spending for various government programs and departments. The power of the purse is a significant aspect of Congressional authority, enabling the legislative branch to influence national priorities and policy directions.

Furthermore, Congress holds the responsibility for oversight of the Executive Branch. Through committees and subcommittees, Congress conducts investigations and hearings, scrutinizing government operations and expenditures. This oversight ensures accountability and transparency in the federal government, fostering an environment where inefficiency and corruption are less likely to thrive.

The Senate has unique responsibilities, including the ratification of treaties and the confirmation of presidential appointments, such as Cabinet members, Supreme Court justices, and federal judges. This advise-and-consent role underscores the Senate's influence in shaping the federal judiciary and in conducting foreign policy.

For immigrants and those seeking to understand the workings of the US government, recognizing the pivotal role of Congress in shaping the country's laws and policies is essential. Congress's actions impact everything from immigration reform to healthcare, education, and environmental policy. Engaging with this process, whether through voting, contacting representatives, or participating in civic activities, is not only a right but a powerful way of making one's voice heard in the corridors of power.

The relationship between Congress and the American populace is dynamic and ever-evolving. As the demographic tapestry of the nation changes, so too do the priorities and concerns that Congress addresses. For those on the path to citizenship, understanding how to effectively engage with Congress is an important step in becoming an active and informed participant in American democracy.

Starting from the premise that every voice matters, Congress in action is a testament to the complex, sometimes messy, but ultimately empowering process of governance in the United States. It offers a fascinating glimpse into the machinery of democracy, where debate, compromise, and decision-making reflect the diverse tapestry of American society.

As you continue to learn about the American government, keep in mind that the structure and functions of Congress are designed to ensure representation and accountability. The legislative process, with its checks and balances, is a fundamental aspect of American democracy that protects the rights and freedoms of all residents, including those on their journey to citizenship.

In summary, the legislative branch plays a critical role in American governance, embodying the principles of democracy through its composition and functions. For immigrants and new citizens, understanding Congress is not just about knowing how laws are made; it's about recognizing the power of participation and the importance of every individual's contribution to the collective story of the United States.

As we delve deeper into the fabric of American government, remember that the story of Congress is a story of people coming together to navigate the challenges and opportunities of a nation. It's about finding common ground and working towards a more perfect union. Your journey to citizenship is a part of this ongoing story, a testament to the enduring strength and promise of American democracy.

The Judicial Branch: Interpreting the Law

Embarking on a journey through the American government structure, we find ourselves at the heart of law and justice - the Judicial Branch. This branch is uniquely poised to interpret and apply the law, ensuring that the constitution's promises are upheld in every courtroom and legal proceeding across the country. We'll explore how this branch shapes the very fabric of American society, touching on its roles, powers, and responsibilities.

The foundation of the Judicial Branch is the United States Constitution itself, which established the Supreme Court as the highest court in the land. However, the constitution leaves significant discretion to Congress to create lower federal courts as needed. This two-tiered system consists of the Supreme Court and a network of Federal Courts, including Circuit Court of Appeals and District Courts. Each has a specific role in interpreting and applying the law, ensuring justice reaches every corner of the nation.

At the apex of this structure sits the Supreme Court, composed of nine Justices, including one Chief Justice and eight Associate Justices.

These individuals are nominated by the President and confirmed by the Senate, holding their positions for life. This lifetime tenure is designed to insulate them from political pressures, allowing them to make decisions based solely on legal merits.

The process through which cases reach the Supreme Court is rigorous and highly selective. The court receives thousands of petitions each year but hears only a fraction that raise significant constitutional questions or legal principles needing clarification. This selective process underscores the court's pivotal role in shaping the country's legal landscape.

Beyond the Supreme Court, the Federal Courts handle a wide variety of cases, including disputes between states, cases involving federal laws, and matters related to treaties and the constitution. These courts serve as the first line of judicial interpretation, applying legislative laws to real-world scenarios.

One of the Judicial Branch's most critical functions is judicial review, the power to invalidate statutes, actions, or regulations from the Executive and Legislative branches that violate the Constitution. This power, established by the landmark case Marbury v. Madison in 1803, ensures that the Constitution remains the supreme law of the land.

The principle of checks and balances is crucial within the American government structure, and the Judicial Branch plays a vital role in this system. It can check the powers of the other two branches, ensuring that laws and executive actions do not overstep constitutional boundaries. This balance of power is fundamental to preserving democracy and protecting individual rights.

Individual rights and freedoms stand at the core of the Judicial Branch's mission. Through landmark rulings on issues such as freedom of speech, civil rights, and privacy, the courts have molded the societal norms that define American life. These decisions are not merely legal pronouncements but echo through generations, shaping public policy and societal values.

Understanding the Judicial Branch's workings, one must recognize its limitations. Courts rely on other government branches to enforce their rulings, possessing neither the sword nor the purse. This reliance on the Executive for enforcement underscores the interdependence of the branches of government, each playing a unique role in governance.

The appointment of Justices and federal judges is often a point of significant interest and contention, highlighting the intersection of law and politics. The President's power to appoint justices, with the Senate's advice and consent, infuses a political element into the judicial system. However, once appointed, justices' commitment to impartiality and the law is paramount, transcending political affiliations.

The impact of the Judicial Branch extends beyond interpreting statutes and constitutional provisions. Its role in social evolution and progress cannot be overstated. Through decisions that have expanded civil liberties and rights, the courts have often been at the forefront of societal change, pushing the nation toward a more inclusive understanding of its founding ideals.

For immigrants and those on the path to citizenship, the Judicial Branch represents a beacon of justice, safeguarding the rights and liberties that attract many to this nation. Understanding its role is not just a matter of civic knowledge but appreciating the protections and opportunities provided under the law.

The journey through the American government's structure, particularly the Judicial Branch, reveals a system designed with checks and balances, aimed at protecting democracy and promoting justice. Its complex, yet fundamental role within the government ensures that laws reflect the constitution's spirit, safeguarding the rights of all individuals, including those seeking to make this country their new home.

As we reflect on the importance of the Judicial Branch, let us be inspired by its commitment to fairness, equality, and justice. These principles are not just the foundation of the American legal system but are pillars that support the dreams and aspirations of all who seek to build a life in the United States. The judiciary's dedication to upholding these ideals reminds us of our collective responsibility to contribute positively to our communities and uphold these values in our daily lives.

In conclusion, the Judicial Branch serves as more than just interpreters of the law; they are guardians of the constitution and protectors of the liberties and rights that define the American experience. As we continue our journey toward understanding the American government structure, let the lessons of the Judicial Branch inspire us to cherish and uphold the principles of democracy, equality, and liberty for all.

CHAPTER 6:
THE ELECTION PROCESS AND
CITIZENSHIP

Embarking on the journey through the landscape of US citizenship unveils the profound role of the election process in shaping the nation's future. This chapter is a compass guiding immigrants through the intricate web of voting rights, the dynamics of political parties, and the electoral system, laying the foundation for informed civic participation. Understanding your voting rights ignites a spark, empowering you to contribute to democracy's flame. Engaging with political parties and navigating the electoral system provides a blueprint for meaningful involvement in shaping policies and making your voice heard. Moreover, the emphasis on civic participation is a call to action, encouraging you to take ownership of your community's wellbeing and the nation's direction. Through active engagement, you become part of something larger than yourself, embodying the spirit of citizenship that has propelled the United States forward throughout its history. This chapter, designed as a beacon, not only prepares you for the USCIS civics test but also inspires you to embrace the responsibilities and joys of American citizenship with confidence and pride.

Understanding Your Voting Rights

Voting is more than a right; it's a pillar of democracy and a powerful way for citizens to influence government decisions. As you make your journey towards US citizenship, understanding the essence of your voting rights illuminates the path to becoming an informed, engaged, and empowered member of the American society.

At its core, the United States is built on the principle that government derives its power from the consent of the governed. This consent is given through the act of voting, a sacred duty that allows citizens to voice their opinions on who should lead and what policies should shape the future of the nation. It's a direct line to the halls of power, from local school boards to the presidency.

Your right to vote as a citizen is protected by several amendments to the US Constitution and various federal laws. Perhaps the most significant among these is the Fifteenth Amendment, which signals that the right to vote cannot be denied on account of race, color, or previous condition of servitude. Following this, the Nineteenth Amendment extended voting rights to women, underscoring the importance of inclusivity in the electoral process.

Furthermore, the Twenty-sixth Amendment lowered the voting age from 21 to 18, expanding the franchise to younger Americans and acknowledging their stake in the country's future. These amendments are milestones in the ongoing journey toward a more inclusive democracy.

Despite these protections, the path to voting has not always been smooth. Throughout history, various obstacles have been placed in the way of potential voters. Understanding these challenges is crucial, not just as a historical lesson but as a reminder of the importance of remaining vigilant in protecting voting rights for everyone.

Voting rights laws, like the Voting Rights Act of 1965, play a pivotal role in combating discrimination and ensuring that everyone's vote counts equally. This landmark legislation was instrumental in eliminating many of the barriers to voting faced by minorities and marginalized groups.

Yet, the battle for accessible voting continues. Current debates around voter ID laws, purging of voter rolls, and access to polling places highlight the ongoing need for advocacy and vigilance to protect the fundamental right to vote.

As a future citizen, it's important to be aware of the various ways in which you can register to vote. Each state has its own set of rules, but generally, opportunities to register online, by mail, or in person are available. Taking the time to understand these processes in your state is the first step towards active participation in elections.

Equally important is educating yourself on the issues and candidates on the ballot. Voting is most impactful when it's informed. Numerous non-partisan resources are available to help voters understand the positions and platforms of candidates and the implications of ballot measures.

Remember, voting doesn't end at the ballot box. Engaging with elected officials, staying informed about ongoing issues, and continuing to participate in civic activities are all part of the broader definition of democratic engagement. Voting is the beginning, not the endpoint, of your civic journey.

Many immigrants have left countries where fair and free elections were not a given. The right to vote in the United States is a precious gift, a hard-earned right that countless individuals have fought to secure and protect. Embracing this right is not just a duty but a tribute to those who have paved the way for democracy to flourish.

When you cast your vote, you're connecting with a tradition that is larger than any single individual—it's a collective exercise of power that shapes the nation's destiny. This act of voting weaves your voice into the American story, making it richer and more representative of its people's diverse tapestry.

As you prepare for your citizenship test and look forward to taking the oath, envision the moment when you'll first exercise your right to vote. It's a significant milestone marking your full embrace of American citizenship. Voting is a testament to the belief in democracy's promise and its continual renewal through the active participation of its citizens.

Remember, every vote counts. The strength of democracy lies in the willingness of its citizens to participate actively in its processes. By voting, you're not just shaping the present; you're laying down the groundwork for future generations. Your vote is your voice, a declaration of your values, and a beacon of hope for a more inclusive, fair, and democratic society.

In closing, as you embark on this final stretch towards becoming a US citizen, let the knowledge of your voting rights inspire you to fully engage in the civic life of your new country. Understand that your vote is a powerful instrument of change, a tool for shaping the policies and leaders that will determine the future of the United States. Welcome the responsibility with enthusiasm and pride, and prepare to make your mark on the great American experiment in democracy.

Political Parties and the Electoral System

In the fabric of American democracy, political parties and the electoral system serve as the warp and weft, intertwining to shape the nation's political landscape. Understanding how these components work together is crucial for those on the path to citizenship, as it empowers you to participate more effectively in your new country's civic life.

The United States primarily operates within a two-party system, with the Democratic Party and the Republican Party at its core. This doesn't mean other parties don't exist or matter, but the majority of elected officials belong to one of these two. Created over time, the two-party system has guided American politics through its history, reflecting the evolving views and values of its people.

Political parties in the U.S. are much more than just groups of people who share similar views. They organize elections, select candidates, and work to get their members elected. They're also responsible for setting policy goals and agendas that reflect their ideologies. The Democrats traditionally advocate for progressive policies and social welfare, while Republicans typically support smaller government and free-market economics.

The electoral system of the U.S. is complex and unique, often puzzling newcomers. It's a representative democracy, where citizens vote for their leaders who then make decisions on their behalf. The most prominent feature of this system is the Electoral College, a process designed to balance the vote's power between smaller and larger states in the presidential election.

At the heart of the electoral system is the principle of majority rule, with the expectation of fair representation for all. To vote in the U.S., one must be a legal citizen, at least 18 years old, and registered under the state's specific requirements. Voting rights were hard-won through centuries of struggle, highlighting the importance of participation in this democratic privilege.

Registration and voting processes vary from state to state, emphasizing the decentralized nature of the electoral system. This variability reflects the country's value of federalism, allowing states to have control over their electoral affairs, so long as they adhere to the Constitution.

Primaries and caucuses are methods political parties use to select their candidates for the general election. Primaries are state-level elections where party members vote for their preferred candidate. Caucuses, on the other hand, are local gathering where members discuss and vote on candidates. These pre-elections play a crucial role in the democratic process, allowing party members to have a say in who represents them.

The General Election, held every four years for the presidency, every two for Congress, and at various intervals for other offices, is the culmination of the electoral process. It's a time when citizens across the nation cast their votes for their chosen representatives, making it one of the most significant acts of civic participation.

Understanding the role of third parties adds depth to one's grasp of the American political landscape. Although the Democratic and Republican parties dominate, third parties such as the Libertarian, Green, and others have shaped policies and debates. They bring to the forefront issues that may be overlooked by the major parties, enriching the democratic dialogue.

The electoral system also includes mechanisms like referendums and initiatives, allowing citizens to vote directly on specific legislation or issues. This direct democracy facet empowers voters to have a direct hand in law-making, highlighting the participatory nature of American government.

Electoral reform is a constant topic of discussion, reflecting the desire of the American people to improve their electoral system. Issues like campaign finance, election security, and the Electoral College's role are continually debated, evidencing the dynamic and evolving nature of U.S. democracy.

An informed citizen is a powerful one. For immigrants aspiring to citizenship, understanding the political parties and electoral system is not just about passing a test; it's about becoming an active, informed participant in America's democratic tradition. It's about making your voice heard and contributing to the community and nation you are joining.

Empowerment comes from knowledge and participation. As you learn more about the U.S. political system, let this knowledge inspire you to become involved in your local community. Whether through voting, volunteering for a campaign, or simply staying informed on political matters, your engagement is a testament to the strength of American democracy.

The journey to U.S. citizenship is steeped in significance—marking not just a change in national identity, but a commitment to the principles that have shaped this nation. Understanding the electoral process and the role of political parties offers a window into the heart of what it means to be an American—a responsibility to oneself and to the wider community to participate, contribute, and uphold the democratic values that bind the nation.

As you prepare for the citizenship test and beyond, let your learning journey extend into an engagement with the political life of your new home. Your participation is a vital thread in the ongoing tapestry of American democracy, enriching it with your unique perspectives and experiences. Welcome to a vital part of your journey toward becoming not just a citizen by law, but by heart—engaged, informed, and contributing to the future of the United States.

The Importance of Civic Participation

Civic participation is the bedrock on which the edifice of any thriving democratic society is built. It is through active engagement in civic life that individuals can collectively shape the destiny of their community, state, and nation. For immigrants pursuing U.S. citizenship, understanding and embracing the concept of civic participation is crucial. It's more than a responsibility; it's an opportunity to contribute to the country's democratic process and ensure that its ideals of liberty, equality, and justice are preserved for generations to come.

Engagement in civic activities encompasses a broad spectrum of actions: from voting in elections to attending city council meetings, from community volunteering to participating in political debates. Each of these actions strengthens the democratic fabric of the society, ensuring that the voices of the people are heard, and their interests are represented.

Voting, the most fundamental form of civic participation, is a powerful tool through which citizens exercise their right to influence government decisions. It is the cornerstone of democracy that allows the electorate to choose their representatives and hold them accountable. Beyond the act of casting a ballot, however, is the imperative to make informed decisions. This necessitates a commitment to staying informed about political, social, and economic issues.

For immigrants, the path to full civic participation begins with naturalization, a process that not only grants them the right to vote but also opens up avenues for deeper engagement in American civic life. By becoming citizens, immigrants affirm their commitment to the United States and its democratic principles. This transition imbues them with a sense of belonging and ownership over their adopted country's fate, encouraging a more active and passionate participation in its democracy.

Civic education is another pivotal aspect of civic participation. Understanding the structure of the U.S. government, the rights and responsibilities of citizenship, and the democratic ideals that guide public policy are essential for meaningful engagement. This educational journey empowers new citizens to navigate the complexities of American politics and contribute effectively to public discourse.

Community service is civic participation's most tangible expression. It is through volunteering and involvement in local initiatives that individuals can directly impact the well-being of their communities. This form of participation fosters a sense of solidarity and collective responsibility, vital for nurturing a caring and equitable society.

It's important to recognize that civic participation also includes being an active part of one's local community in informal ways. Social interactions, cultural exchanges, and mutual support among neighbors strengthen communal bonds and promote inclusivity and understanding. For immigrants, these interactions are invaluable opportunities for cultural assimilation and personal growth.

Advocacy and activism are equally integral to civic participation. They enable individuals and groups to champion causes, influence public policy, and effect social change. Through peaceful protest, petitioning, and community organizing, citizens can address inequalities, defend their rights, and advocate for others.

Digital platforms have transformed civic participation, offering new avenues for engagement and activism. Social media, online forums, and digital petitions allow individuals to express their opinions, mobilize support, and connect with like-minded members of society. For immigrants, who might be navigating linguistic and cultural barriers, these platforms can serve as vital tools for participation and advocacy.

Engaging with the electoral system beyond voting — such as campaign volunteering or running for office — is another powerful form of civic participation. These actions not only contribute to the democratic process but also ensure that the government reflects the diversity of the American populace. For immigrants, who bring fresh perspectives and experiences, engaging in this way can be particularly impactful.

Educational institutions play a critical role in fostering civic participation among young citizens and immigrants alike. Schools and colleges are not just centers of academic learning; they are places where the seeds of civic responsibility are sown. Through civic education programs, students learn the importance of participation and are equipped with the skills needed to be active, informed members of society.

It's also essential to acknowledge barriers to civic participation, such as language difficulties, lack of information, and economic constraints. Overcoming these challenges requires a concerted effort from individuals, communities, and governmental bodies to ensure that all citizens, regardless of their background, have the opportunity to participate fully in the democratic process.

Enhancing civic participation among immigrants involves providing spaces where their voices can be heard and their contributions recognized. Community centers, cultural organizations, and political forums should be welcoming spaces for immigrants to share their experiences, connect with others, and enrich the societal tapestry with their unique backgrounds and perspectives.

Lastly, civic participation is a cycle that nurtures itself — the more people engage, the healthier and more vibrant their democracy becomes. When citizens see the tangible results of their involvement, it reinforces the value of their contribution and spurs further participation. For immigrants, this positive feedback loop affirms their role in, and commitment to, their new homeland.

In conclusion, civic participation is not just a duty of citizenship; it is a privilege and an honor. It is through active involvement in the civic life of their adopted country that immigrants can fully realize the American dream. By voting, volunteering, engaging in community life, and advocating for societal betterment, they not only enrich their lives but also contribute to the ongoing narrative of American democracy. The path to citizenship is both a personal journey and a collective endeavor — by participating in the civic fabric of the nation, immigrants weave their threads into the American tapestry, ensuring its strength, vibrancy, and resilience for generations to come.

CHAPTER 7:
RIGHTS AND RESPONSIBILITIES OF CITIZENS

Stepping into Chapter 7, we explore the vital role every citizen plays in the fabric of American society, delving into the balance of rights and responsibilities that form the cornerstone of U.S. citizenship. Embracing your role as a citizen isn't just about reveling in the freedoms and protections offered; it's equally about shouldering the civic duties and responsibilities vital for the nation's wellbeing. From understanding your fundamental rights enshrined in the Constitution to participating actively in community and volunteer efforts, this chapter serves as a guiding light towards impactful citizenship. It's a journey that promises not just personal growth but also deepens your connection to the community and the nation at large. By participating in democracy, respecting the law, paying taxes, serving on a jury when called, and understanding the power of your vote, you contribute to the country's success and uphold the principles it stands on. Let's dive into the essence of what it means to be a citizen, highlighting the mutual respect between individuals' freedoms and their duties to community and country. This understanding is not just crucial for those preparing for the USCIS civics test but enlightening for anyone looking to grasp the full spectrum of American citizenship.

Know Your Rights: Freedom and Protections

Welcome to a vital section dedicated to illuminating the freedoms and protections guaranteed to you as a future citizen of the United States.

This journey through understanding your rights is more than just a preparatory step for the USCIS civics test; it's an essential foundation for your life in the USA. The rights enshrined within the Constitution and its amendments are not merely historical words; they are living promises that ensure your liberty, dignity, and pursuit of happiness.

At the heart of these rights is the Bill of Rights, the first ten amendments to the Constitution, which collectively safeguard the individual freedoms and legal protections of all Americans. These amendments cover a broad spectrum of rights, from the freedom of speech and religion to the right to a fair trial and protection against unreasonable searches and seizures. Each right plays a pivotal role in maintaining the democratic fabric of the nation and empowering its citizens.

The First Amendment famously protects the freedom of speech, the press, religion, assembly, and the right to petition the government. This cornerstone of American democracy allows you to express your thoughts, critique the government, practice your faith, gather for peaceful protests, and seek remedies for grievances without fear of retribution. It's this freedom that fuels innovation, creativity, and social progress.

Equally important is the right to privacy, though not explicitly mentioned in the Constitution, it has been interpreted through various amendments, including the Fourth, which guards against unwarranted searches and seizures. This protection ensures that your personal space, belongings, and communications remain safe from intrusion, upholding the dignity and autonomy of every individual.

The Fifth through Eighth Amendments detail rights related to criminal proceedings, such as the right to remain silent, the guarantee of a speedy and public trial by jury, and protection against cruel and unusual punishment. These provisions ensure that justice is both fair and humane, reflecting the nation's commitment to individual rights even in the face of misconduct.

Another vital protection is the Right to Vote, enshrined in several amendments (the 15th, 19th, 24th, and 26th) which collectively ensure that the right to vote cannot be denied on account of race, color, previous condition of servitude, sex, failing to pay any tax, or age for those 18 years and older. Voting is the most direct way you can influence how your community, state, and country are governed.

It's essential to recognize the role of the Fourteenth Amendment in all of this. It not only guarantees equal protection under the laws but also extends the protections in the Bill of Rights to apply at the state level. This means state governments are also prohibited from infringing on your individual rights. Its significance cannot be overstated, as it ensures that these freedoms follow you across all 50 states.

Understanding your rights also means recognizing your responsibility to respect the rights of others. The fabric of a peaceful and progressive society is woven from mutual respect and understanding. While you are empowered to express your beliefs, this freedom comes with the responsibility to engage in discourse that uplifts and does not harm others.

It's also vital to be aware of how your rights can be lawfully limited. For instance, the freedom of speech does not permit acts of slander, libel, or threats of violence. Recognizing these bounds is crucial in navigating the balance between personal freedoms and the overall well-being of the community.

As immigrants, the journey to full citizenship allows you to contribute to and shape the identity of the United States. Your diverse backgrounds, experiences, and voices add to the multicultural tapestry that is a hallmark of American society. Embracing your rights also means taking up the mantle of responsibility that comes with them—

actively participating in civic duties, from voting to jury service, and contributing to the community.

This section not only aims to prepare you for the USCIS civics test but to also inspire a deep appreciation for the rights and freedoms you will enjoy as an American citizen. It's a powerful reminder that citizenship is not just a status but a privilege that carries with it the potential to make meaningful contributions to the nation's legacy.

In closing, remember that understanding your rights and the protections afforded to you is the first step towards exercising them wisely and with confidence. As you stand on the cusp of becoming a U.S. citizen, take pride in the journey you've undertaken and the role you will play in the ongoing story of democracy and freedom that defines the United States of America.

Your path to citizenship is not just a personal achievement but a testament to the enduring promise of the American Dream. As you continue to learn and grow within this great nation, may you find in your rights not just the freedom to pursue your own happiness but the inspiration to contribute to the welfare and prosperity of all Americans.

Embrace this journey with an open heart and an eager mind, for the rights and freedoms you're soon to fully embrace are the very essence of what it means to be an American. Welcome to a life of liberty, opportunity, and unity. Welcome to your rights and protections as a citizen of the United States of America.

Civic Duties and Responsibilities

Understanding your civic duties and responsibilities is pivotal as you journey towards becoming a United States citizen. It's not just about having rights; it's about actively participating in the democratic process and contributing to the welfare of the community and the nation at large. You are about to embrace a role that is both enriching and demanding.

First and foremost, voting is not just a right; it's a civic duty. Participating in federal, state, and local elections is a direct way to have your voice heard and influence the directions your community and country take. It's a powerful tool of democracy where you get to stand up for what you believe in and support the leaders and policies that align with your values.

Serving on a jury is another fundamental duty of citizenship. When called upon, you play a critical role in maintaining the integrity of the legal system, ensuring that justice is served fairly and impartially. It's a duty that underscores the principle of being judged by a jury of one's peers, a cornerstone of American justice.

Abiding by the law goes without saying. Laws are established to protect the rights and safety of individuals and communities. Following them is paramount to ensuring a peaceful and orderly society. But understand that your responsibility extends beyond just obedience. It's about understanding these laws and why they exist because informed citizens are empowered citizens.

Paying taxes is often met with groans, but it's a responsibility that fuels the country's progress. Taxes fund public services and infrastructure, education, and healthcare, contributing to the common good. Seeing taxes as an investment in your community and country can shift the perspective on this duty.

Defending the country if needed may seem daunting, but it speaks to the profound commitment one makes when becoming a citizen. While not everyone will serve in the military, understanding the sacrifice many have made for freedom is vital. It fosters a sense of gratitude and respect for the protections and liberties enjoyed today.

Another critical aspect of civic responsibility is staying informed about local and national issues. It means looking beyond headlines, understanding the complexities of problems, and being aware of how governmental decisions affect you and your community. An informed citizenry is the backbone of a thriving democracy.

Respecting the rights, beliefs, and opinions of others is essential in a diverse society like the United States. It's what allows democracy to flourish. Constructive dialogues and discussions, even with those whom you disagree, strengthen the community bonds and foster mutual understanding and respect.

Community service is a powerful way to give back. Volunteering doesn't just help those in need; it enriches your life, providing a sense of purpose and connection. It's about recognizing that everyone has something to contribute to the greater good.

Protecting and enjoying the nation's natural resources responsibly ensures that future generations can enjoy them too. From national parks to local green spaces, being stewards of the environment is a testament to the value placed on preserving natural beauty and biodiversity.

Engaging with your community through local organizations or town hall meetings is about taking a proactive stance. It's where your voice, concerns, and ideas can directly contribute to shaping the community's future. This level of engagement demonstrates a commitment to the place you call home.

Educating yourself and others about the Constitution, the Bill of Rights, and the democratic process is foundational. These documents are not just historical texts; they are living promises that outline the rights and duties of every citizen. Sharing this knowledge fosters a more engaged and informed citizenry.

Respecting diversity and promoting equality are values that enrich communities and the nation. Acknowledging and celebrating differences in culture, religion, and backgrounds is a testament to the strength found in diversity. It's about building a society where everyone feels valued and included.

Finally, remember that your journey as a citizen is ongoing. Citizenship is not a destination but a path of continuous engagement, learning, and growth. It's about striving to be an active participant in the democratic process, contributing to the evolving story of the United States.

Embracing your civic duties and responsibilities is a profound endeavor. It's an opportunity to contribute to the welfare and progress of the country actively. With rights come responsibilities, and by fulfilling these, you become an integral part of the living, breathing fabric of American democracy. Welcome to this journey—a journey that not only defines your place in this great nation but also shapes its future.

Community Contribution and Volunteering

As new or future citizens of this great nation, embracing the responsibility of community contribution and volunteering is as vital as understanding the rights that protect us. This section will explore the essence and impact of giving back to the communities we call home, a fundamental aspect of American life that knits the fabric of our society closer together.

Volunteering is more than an act of charity; it's an investment in the well-being of our communities and, by extension, ourselves. The American ethos is steeped in a spirit of self-reliance, community support, and mutual help. From the early days of barn raisings to today's neighborhood cleanups and food drives, Americans have long understood that by lifting each other, we all rise.

Engaging in community service provides a unique opportunity to make a tangible difference in our local areas. Whether it's helping at a local food bank, mentoring a child, or participating in beautification projects, these actions contribute to the vibrant, healthy communities that we all aspire to live in.

The beauty of volunteering lies in its accessibility to all. It does not discriminate by age, race, gender, or socioeconomic status. Everyone has something valuable to contribute, whether it's time, skills, or resources. Recognizing and utilizing these personal assets for the betterment of others is a powerful expression of citizenship.

Furthermore, volunteering fosters a sense of belonging and connection. For immigrants, in particular, volunteering can pave the way for integrating into new communities, understanding cultural nuances, and forming lasting bonds with fellow residents. It's an avenue to not only give back but also to establish oneself within the broader American narrative.

In terms of civic responsibility, volunteering is a practical demonstration of democracy in action. It's about being proactive in addressing community needs and challenges rather than waiting for governmental solutions. This proactive stance is essential in a democracy, where citizens are the primary agents of change and progress.

Education about local governance and community needs is a critical component of effective volunteering. Engaging with community leaders, attending town hall meetings, and staying informed about local issues can enhance the impact of your volunteering efforts. Informed volunteers are empowered volunteers.

The social benefits of volunteering are immense. It creates networks of people with shared interests and values, which can enhance social cohesion and reduce isolation. For many, these networks can provide support in times of personal difficulty, job opportunities, and even lifelong friendships.

Volunteering also offers personal growth opportunities. It challenges individuals to step out of their comfort zones, learn new skills, and take on leadership roles. These experiences can be incredibly enriching, increasing self-confidence, and providing a sense of achievement and purpose.

Economically, the value of volunteer work to communities is immeasurable. The countless hours dedicated to volunteering each year contribute to the quality of life in communities and the efficient functioning of many non-profit organizations and public services. This economic impact, though often unquantified, is profound.

It's important to note that volunteering should not be seen as a one-off activity but as a sustained commitment. Consistent contribution over time amplifies the positive outcomes for both the community and the volunteer. It's about building long-term partnerships that evolve to meet changing community needs.

To those who might feel unsure about where to start, numerous resources are available. Local community centers, non-profits, and online platforms offer a wide range of volunteering opportunities tailored to different interests, skills, and time commitments. Everyone has a place in the world of volunteering.

As you step forward into this journey of community contribution, remember that every small act of volunteering adds up to a greater sum of change. Your efforts, no matter how modest they might seem, have the potential to touch lives and transform communities.

In conclusion, volunteering and community contribution are among the highest expressions of citizenship in the United States. They reflect the core values that have shaped this nation: compassion, cooperation, and civic engagement. As you continue your path towards US citizenship, embrace these opportunities to contribute. Your participation not only enriches your life but helps uphold the ideals that make this country truly exceptional.

Let this section be a launching pad for your involvement in community service. Take the step, big or small, towards making a difference. The impact of your actions will resonate far beyond what you can see, weaving your story into the American tapestry of community and mutual support.

CHAPTER 8:
IMPORTANT SYMBOLS AND LANDMARKS

Embarking on a journey to understand the essence of the United States, it's pivotal to grasp the meanings behind its revered symbols and landmarks. These symbols, from the majestic Statue of Liberty standing tall in New York Harbor symbolizing freedom and democracy, to the solemn grounds of Gettysburg, remind us of the sacrifices made for liberty. Each landmark tells a story, contributing to the complex narrative of the nation. The American flag, with its stripes representing the original 13 colonies and stars symbolizing the 50 states, serves as a beacon of unity and perseverance through adversity. These symbols and landmarks aren't just emblems of past events; they are living reminders that continue to inspire and unite Americans. They echo the enduring principles upon which the nation was founded and serve as a compass guiding its future. By delving into the stories behind these national treasures, immigrants and citizens alike can foster a deeper connection with the country and gain insight into the values it holds dear. This chapter not only educates but also motivates readers to further explore the rich tapestry of American history and civics, empowering them on their path to citizenship. It's a testament to the idea that understanding and appreciating these symbols is a step towards embodying the spirit of the nation, a crucial aspect of the journey to becoming an informed and engaged U.S. citizen.

National Symbols and Their Meanings

Embarking on the journey to understand the United States more deeply involves exploring its national symbols. These symbols act as beacons of the nation's identity, history, and values. They're more than just icons; they are the threads in the fabric of American society that tie past to present and future. Let's delve into these symbols and uncover their inherent meanings and the roles they play in uniting a diverse populace.

The American flag, known as the Stars and Stripes, is perhaps the most recognizable national symbol. Its 13 stripes represent the original colonies that declared independence from Britain, while the 50 stars symbolize the states that make up the Union today. The flag embodies freedom, bravery, and patriotism. When we see it flying high, it's a reminder of the sacrifices made for liberty and the ongoing commitment to uphold democratic values.

The Bald Eagle, the national bird, stands for strength, longevity, and resilience. Chosen in 1782 as a symbol because of its long life and majestic appearance, the eagle reflects America's sovereignty and its place in the world. The sight of a Bald Eagle soaring high in the sky sparks a sense of pride and a reminder of the nation's ability to rise above challenges.

The Liberty Bell, with its infamous crack, tells a story of America's fight for freedom. Originally rung to mark the reading of the Declaration of Independence, it now symbolizes liberty and justice for all. The bell invites contemplation on the principles that founded the nation and encourages all to work towards ensuring these freedoms remain intact.

The Statue of Liberty stands tall, not just as a monument but as a symbol of hope and democracy. Gifted by France in 1886, Lady Liberty welcomes everyone, regardless of where they come from, with open arms. The torch she carries is a beacon of enlightenment, illuminating the path to freedom and opportunity.

The National Anthem, "The Star-Spangled Banner," evokes a deep sense of patriotism when sung at events nationwide. Its lyrics, inspired by the sight of the American flag still waving after a night of bombardment during the War of 1812, remind citizens of the resilience and unity required to safeguard their country.

The Great Seal of the United States, with its eagle, olive branch, and arrows, encapsulates peace and readiness to defend. The seal's design reflects the country's determination to prefer peace but its readiness for war if necessary to protect its people and their freedoms.

The motto "E Pluribus Unum," found on the Great Seal and various U.S. currency, translates to "Out of many, one." This motto celebrates America's diversity and the strength found in coming together as a nation, united by shared values and dreams.

In addition to these symbols, the Pledge of Allegiance serves as a verbal affirmation of loyalty to the United States. Reciting it, citizens and aspiring citizens alike commit themselves to the ideals of the republic, promising unity and respect for the flag and what it represents.

The White House, as the residence of the President, stands as a potent symbol of the American government's executive branch. It signifies leadership and the responsibility carried by those elected to lead, embodying the nation's democratic principles and the public's trust.

Mount Rushmore, with the sculpted heads of four revered presidents, symbolizes the foundational ideals of democracy, freedom, and the struggle for human rights. It's a monument to leadership, inspiration, and the American spirit, emphasizing the importance of exemplary governance and the impact of steadfast leaders.

The United States currency, from the imagery chosen for coins and bills to the phrases inscribed, is imbued with national values and historical figures who embody specific aspects of the country's identity. Through these symbols, the narrative of hard work, innovation, and perseverance is told.

The holidays celebrated, such as Independence Day and Memorial Day, are embodiments of America's values, signifying independence, sacrifice, and gratitude for the freedoms enjoyed today. These days foster a united national community, remembrance, and a re-invigoration of patriotic spirit.

The National Parks, preserved and treasured, are symbols of America's natural beauty and its commitment to conserving the environment for future generations. They remind us of the country's vastness and the importance of protecting natural wonders.

The American Rose, designated as the national floral emblem, symbolizes beauty, love, and the growth blossoming from care and dedication. It reflects the nation's cultural appreciation for nature and the arts, emphasizing the importance of nurturing growth and beauty in all forms.

Understanding these symbols and their meanings enriches the journey to citizenship by connecting individuals with the nation's heritage and values. Each symbol tells part of the United States' story, inviting everyone to reflect on their role in continuing its legacy. As you prepare for the USCIS civics test and your eventual citizenship, remember that these symbols represent not just the history of the nation but the shared future you are stepping into.

Historic Landmarks and Their Stories

The USA is sprinkled with historic landmarks, each telling a unique story of the nation's journey. These sites are not just tourist destinations but are pivotal in understanding America's evolution. This section delves into some of these landmarks and the remarkable stories they tell, a testament to the resilience, courage, and innovation that define the United States.

Liberty Island in New York City is home to one of the most iconic symbols of freedom, the Statue of Liberty. Gifted by France in 1886, this colossal neoclassical sculpture stands tall, welcoming millions who come in search of freedom and opportunity. It's not just a monument but a beacon of hope, representing liberty and democracy globally.

On the other end of the spectrum lies the solemn ground of Gettysburg, Pennsylvania. The site of the Gettysburg Battle, a turning point in the Civil War, now serves as a reminder of the cost of unity and equality. The Gettysburg Address, delivered by President Abraham Lincoln, redefined the purpose of the war and the very essence of American democracy, emphasizing "government of the people, by the people, for the people."

Moving westward, the Gateway Arch in St. Louis, Missouri, celebrates the country's expansion west. Known as the "Gateway to the West," this stainless steel monument honors the pioneers of the nineteenth century who ventured into unknown territories, shaping the nation's destiny.

Another landmark that speaks volumes of the American spirit is Independence Hall in Philadelphia, Pennsylvania. It was here that both the Declaration of Independence and the United States Constitution were debated and adopted, laying the groundwork for the nation's governance and asserting its independence from British rule.

The freedom struggle is further immortalized at the Lincoln Memorial in Washington, D.C. This monument honors Abraham Lincoln, the 16th President, who led the nation through the Civil War and worked to abolish slavery. The memorial has also been a backdrop to many significant civil rights movements, including Martin Luther King Jr.'s iconic "I Have a Dream" speech.

Not all landmarks are created by human achievements; some are nature's own. The Grand Canyon in Arizona is a testament to the natural beauty and grandeur of the United States. Carved by the Colorado River, this geological marvel is a reminder of nature's power and the importance of preserving our environment for future generations.

In Boston, Massachusetts, the Freedom Trail weaves through the city, linking 16 historic sites that were pivotal in the quest for independence. Walking this trail is like stepping back in time, getting a firsthand experience of the American Revolution's brave struggle for freedom against colonial rule.

The National Mall in Washington, D.C., is a unique landmark, serving as the stage for American democracy. This open park area, surrounded by the country's important institutions like the Capitol, White House, and various museums, hosts celebrations, protests, and gatherings, reflecting the vibrant and participatory nature of American democracy.

Ellis Island, in the shadow of the Statue of Liberty, served as the nation's busiest immigrant inspection station from 1892 to 1954. Today, the Ellis Island Immigration Museum tells the stories of the millions who came through its doors, seeking a new beginning in America. It stands as a symbol of the nation's diverse heritage and the enduring promise of the American Dream.

Another poignant reminder of the struggles for civil rights is the Birmingham Civil Rights National Monument in Alabama. This area, including the 16th Street Baptist Church, where a tragic bombing killed four young girls, serves as a sober reminder of the fight against racial segregation and for the equality that defines the spirit of modern America.

Mount Rushmore National Memorial in South Dakota features the colossal carvings of the faces of four US Presidents: George

Washington, Thomas Jefferson, Theodore Roosevelt, and Abraham Lincoln. This monument captures the essence of American leadership and the founding ideals of freedom, democracy, and the pursuit of happiness.

The Alamo in San Antonio, Texas, is a historic Spanish mission and fortress compound famous for the Battle of the Alamo during the Texas Revolution. It symbolizes the heroic resistance of a small group against overwhelming odds and is a shrine of Texas liberty.

In Montgomery, Alabama, the Rosa Parks Library and Museum commemorates the "Mother of the Freedom Movement," Rosa Parks. Her refusal to give up her bus seat ignited the Montgomery Bus Boycott and became a pivotal moment in the fight against racial segregation.

Lastly, the United States Capitol in Washington, D.C., is not just an architectural marvel but the heart of American democracy, where laws are made, leaders are chosen, and the ideals of democracy are put into action. Its dome, standing tall, is a symbol of the nation's resilience and commitment to democratic principles.

These landmarks, each with their own story, are chapters in the larger American narrative. They inspire us with lessons from the past, reminding us of the struggles and triumphs that have shaped the United States. As future citizens, it's essential to understand these symbols not just for the citizenship test but to appreciate the values they embody. They are reminders of the enduring strength of freedom, democracy, and the pursuit of a more perfect union.

CHAPTER 9:
INSIGHT INTO AMERICAN SOCIETY

In the tapestry of global cultures, the American society stands out as a vibrant mosaic of cultural diversity and value systems, grounded in the pursuit of freedom and the promise of opportunity for all. As we delve into the societal norms and cultural dynamics, it becomes evident that the fabric of American society is woven with threads of resilience, innovation, and a steadfast commitment to the principles of democracy. Education and work in the USA mirror the society's hustle for advancement and self-improvement, highlighting the unequivocal belief in the power of knowledge and hard work. Yet, beneath the surface of these achievements, social issues and public opinion reflect the ongoing dialogues and challenges that shape the nation's conscience. Engaging with these elements provides invaluable insights into the complexities of American life, empowering immigrants and those on their journey to citizenship to navigate the social landscape with awareness and empathy. Embracing the diversity and participating actively in the societal discourse is not only a step towards integration but a stride towards contributing to the community's growth and enrichment.

Cultural Diversity and American Values

The mosaic of American society is a vibrant tapestry woven with threads of cultural diversity and a shared commitment to fundamental values. This rich tapestry, emblematic of the nation's identity, underscores the principle that while we may come from different backgrounds, we are united in our pursuit of life, liberty, and happiness.

The concept of cultural diversity in the United States is not just a modern phenomenon but a foundational aspect that has been shaping the country since its inception.

At the heart of American values is the belief in freedom and democracy. These principles serve as the bedrock upon which the nation was built and continue to inspire those who come to its shores seeking a new beginning. The respect for individual rights, the rule of law, and the idea that everyone deserves an equal opportunity to succeed are ingrained in the American ethos. Such values invite a symphony of perspectives, encouraging open dialogue and mutual respect among the country's diverse population.

The story of American cultural diversity is also the story of immigration. From the early settlers to the huddled masses arriving at Ellis Island, and the waves of immigrants landing at airports today, the United States has been a beacon of hope for countless individuals across the globe. This continuous influx of people from different cultures has greatly enriched American society, introducing a wealth of traditions, languages, and cuisines that have become part of the American experience.

Education plays a pivotal role in fostering understanding and appreciation for cultural diversity. Schools across the country often celebrate cultural heritage months, host international festivals, and incorporate multicultural education into their curriculum. This emphasis on educational inclusivity helps to cultivate an environment where young Americans learn to embrace diversity not as a challenge, but as an invaluable asset.

Workplace diversity is another area where American values shine. Companies nationwide recognize the benefits of a diverse workforce, including increased innovation, better decision-making, and a broader customer base. By valuing diversity, businesses mirror the nation's principles of equal opportunity and contribute to a more inclusive society.

Despite the progress, the journey towards a fully inclusive society continues. The United States grapples with social issues that challenge its ideals of equality and justice for all. Discrimination, racism, and inequality persist, sparking movements and debates aimed at addressing these problems. It's a complex journey, reflective of a nation always in motion—striving to fulfill its promise of liberty and justice for everyone.

The celebration of cultural diversity in America is evident in the vibrant festivals, religious observances, and community events that take place throughout the year. These celebrations are not only opportunities for fun and fellowship but also moments for reflection on the country's journey towards inclusivity and mutual respect.

Literature and the arts serve as conduits for understanding and expressing the country's multifaceted identity. American literature, music, film, and visual arts are replete with examples of how cultural diversity has influenced and enriched the creative domain, offering insights into the complexities and beauty of the human experience.

Food is another powerful expression of cultural diversity. The American culinary landscape is a testament to the nation's melting pot, with dishes from around the world becoming staples on the American dining table. This fusion of flavors not only satisfies the palate but also serves as a delicious reminder of the country's diverse heritage.

Language diversity further exemplifies the multicultural fabric of American society. While English is the de facto language, communities across the nation speak a multitude of languages, reflecting the rich linguistic heritage of their inhabitants. Efforts to preserve these languages and promote bilingual education underscore the value placed on linguistic diversity.

The concept of the "American Dream" is intrinsically linked to the nation's diversity. It is the belief that regardless of one's background, every individual has the potential for success through hard work and determination. This dream is a unifying aspiration, embodying the hope and opportunities that have drawn people to the United States for centuries.

American values of freedom, equality, and opportunity are not just ideals but lived experiences that evolve with each generation. As new citizens contribute their voices and stories, they enrich the narrative of American democracy, underscoring the nation's enduring commitment to being a land of opportunity for all.

In embracing cultural diversity, America acknowledges that its strength lies in its differences, not despite them. This recognition fosters a sense of belonging and community among individuals, reinforcing the idea that everyone has a role to play in the ongoing story of the nation.

The American spirit of innovation and resilience is fueled by its diversity. By drawing on the talents, perspectives, and experiences of its people, the United States continues to lead in many fields, demonstrating the power of inclusion and diversity.

Cultural diversity and American values are inextricably linked, each shaping and strengthening the other. As the United States moves forward, it carries with it the promise of a more inclusive society, where diversity is celebrated as a vital component of the American identity. The journey towards fully realizing these values is ongoing, but the commitment to pursuing them remains a defining characteristic of the American experience.

Education and Work in the USA

Understanding the landscape of education and workforce in the United States is a fundamental step toward integrating into American society and seizing the opportunities it offers. The education system here is designed to provide a wide range of learning opportunities, fostering not only academic skills but also critical thinking and creativity. From public schools to prestigious universities, the U.S. education system aims to equip students with the knowledge and competencies they need to succeed in a rapidly changing world.

The public education system in the USA is managed at the state level, offering kindergarten through 12th grade at no cost. Each state sets its own educational standards and relies on property taxes for funding, which can lead to disparities in the quality of education between different districts. Nevertheless, the aim is universal—to prepare students for life beyond the classroom, whether that involves further education or entering the workforce.

Higher education in the United States is renowned worldwide, boasting institutions like Harvard, MIT, and Stanford among its ranks. However, college education can come with a significant cost, leading many students to seek financial aid through scholarships, grants, and loans. The investment in higher education is often seen as a pathway to better job prospects and a more secure future.

The workforce in the U.S. is just as diverse as its population, with a wide range of industries from technology and finance to healthcare and education. The American work culture emphasizes hard work, ambition, and innovation, with a strong belief in the possibility of upward mobility through personal effort. Networking and ongoing education are commonly encouraged as means to advance one's career.

Immigrants play a critical role in the U.S. workforce, bringing unique skills and perspectives that contribute to the country's economic dynamism. They are represented across all sectors, often filling gaps in the labor market and driving innovation. Recognizing the value of this diversity, many employers are committed to inclusive hiring practices and supporting the integration of immigrants into the work-force.

Despite the opportunities, navigating the job market in the U.S. can be challenging for newcomers. Differences in language, cultural expectations, and professional norms can create barriers to employment. English as a Second Language (ESL) programs and workforce development initiatives are essential resources that help bridge this gap, offering language tutoring and professional training geared toward the needs of immigrants.

Entrepreneurship is another hallmark of the American economy, with the country being known as the land of opportunity. The spirit of innovation and risk-taking is celebrated and supported by an ecosystem that fosters startup growth, including access to capital, mentorship, and a network of entrepreneurial peers. Immigrants have been at the forefront of founding some of the most successful American companies, showcasing the potential for achievement regardless of one's background.

Work-life balance is an evolving concept in the US, with increasing awareness of the importance of mental health and well-being. Many employers now offer flexible working arrangements, wellness programs, and support for families in response to demands for a more balanced approach to work and life.

Legal rights in the workplace are also an important aspect of working in the USA. Laws at the federal and state level protect employees from discrimination, ensure a minimum wage, and regulate hours and conditions of work. Being familiar with these rights is crucial for all workers, including immigrants, to ensure fair treatment and safe working conditions.

The path to successful integration into the U.S. workforce often involves education—formal or informal. Continuous learning and adaptability are key traits that employers value, encouraging workers to pursue professional development and further education throughout their careers. Community colleges, online courses, and vocational training programs offer opportunities for skill advancement and career changes, aligning with the needs of a rapidly evolving job market.

The intersection of education and work in the USA is dynamic, reflecting the broader trends of globalization and technological advancement. As the economy shifts towards knowledge-based industries, the demand for higher education and specialized skills will continue to grow.

For immigrants, the journey to achieving the American Dream often starts with understanding and navigating the educational and work environments. It's a path that requires persistence, resilience, and adaptability but promises rewarding opportunities for growth and contribution to society.

Engagement with local communities and participation in social and civic life further enriches the immigrant experience, providing avenues for meaningful connections and mutual learning. It's not just about individual success but also about contributing to the vibrant, diverse fabric of American society.

Finally, remember that success in the USA is not solely measured by academic achievements or career milestones but also by the ability to adapt, overcome challenges, and make a positive impact in one's community. Each journey is unique, but the pursuit of education and meaningful work is a common dream that unites people from all backgrounds in the quest for a better life in America.

The stories of those who have navigated the complexities of education and work in the USA are a testament to the resilience and diversity that characterize American society. As you embark on or continue your journey, draw inspiration from these stories, and look forward to adding your own chapter in the ongoing narrative of the American Dream.

Social Issues and Public Opinion

The landscape of American society is ever-changing, a dynamic interplay of cultures, ideas, and opinions that shape the national conscience. Social issues and public opinion are intricately linked, influencing policies, elections, and the very fabric of daily life. As future citizens and current residents, understanding these social issues offers not just insight into America's challenges and achievements but also a path to active, informed participation in its democracy.

In the heart of public discourse, issues such as immigration, healthcare, and education evoke strong opinions and are pivotal to understanding the priorities of the American people. Immigration, a foundational component of America's history, remains a complex and contentious topic. It shapes the nation's demographics, economy, and identity, sparking debates on policy and human rights.

Healthcare, universally important to all residents, reflects the nation's values and its struggles with equity, quality, and cost. The debate over healthcare reform touches on fundamental questions about the role of government and the rights of citizens to access care.

Education is another cornerstone of societal well-being and mobility, directly impacting the nation's future. Discussions on educational equity, student debt, and school reform highlight the challenges and opportunities in nurturing a diverse, skilled populace.

Economic inequality, a rising worry among many Americans, prompts conversations about the distribution of wealth, opportunities for upward mobility, and support for those in need. The American Dream, while still a key narrative, is scrutinized through the realities of socioeconomic barriers and changing economic landscapes.

Civil rights issues, including racial equality, gender equity, and LGBTQ+ rights, are at the forefront of America's journey towards a more inclusive democracy. Efforts to address systemic inequalities and protect individual freedoms define both progress and resistance in the nation's evolution.

The environment and climate change represent an increasingly prominent public concern. Debates over policies to address global warming, conservation efforts, and sustainable energy sources are critical to both the country's and the planet's future.

Technology and privacy issues have gained prominence in the digital age, challenging traditional notions of security, freedom, and ethics. Americans grapple with the balance between innovation and the protection of individual rights in a world of pervasive technology.

The concept of national security, encompassing both military and cybersecurity concerns, remains a priority in public opinion and government policy. Events that affect the nation's safety and its role on the global stage are closely followed by the American public.

On the political front, partisanship and polarization present challenges to governance and civil discourse. The increasing divide between political ideologies impacts families, communities, and the legislative process, underscoring the importance of dialogue and understanding in a pluralistic society.

Public health, particularly in the wake of the COVID-19 pandemic, has become a central issue. The crisis and its management have highlighted strengths and vulnerabilities in the healthcare system, economy, and social safety nets, prompting reassessment and innovation in public policy.

The fight against misinformation and the pursuit of truth and transparency in media and government underscore the critical role of an informed electorate. As digital platforms evolve, so too does the landscape of information, requiring vigilance and critical thinking from citizens.

Gun control and the rights of gun ownership continue to generate passionate debate, reflecting deeper values around personal freedom, safety, and the interpretation of the Constitution. This issue exemplifies the complexity of balancing rights and responsibilities in a free society.

Homelessness and housing insecurity, exacerbated by economic pressures and health crises, highlight the need for compassionate and effective solutions to support the most vulnerable populations and ensure the stability and dignity of all citizens.

In summary, the social issues that animate public opinion in the United States are diverse and multifaceted. They invite engagement, debate, and action, offering both challenges and opportunities for those navigating the path to citizenship and participation in American life. Understanding and contributing to these conversations not only enriches individual experience but also strengthens the fabric of the nation.

CHAPTER 10:
ECONOMIC UNDERSTANDING: THE US MARKET

As we delve into the heart of the American economy, it's crucial to recognize the intricate tapestry that makes up the US market. This chapter is dedicated to unraveling the complexities of economic principles, operations, and structures that sustain one of the world's most dynamic economies. Embracing an economic understanding is not merely about grasping facts and figures; it's about perceiving the broader picture of how market forces shape the everyday lives of people and the nation's destiny. From the significance of the basics of the American economy, to the pivotal role taxes and personal finance play in the fabric of societal health and individual prosperity, this chapter illuminates the pathways through which the economy operates and influences the American dream. With the empowerment of knowledge, immigrants and readers from all walks of life can make informed decisions, participate more fully in economic opportunities, and foster a vibrant community that upholds the values of hard work, innovation, and shared prosperity. As we explore the US market's foundations, mechanisms, and impacts, let this chapter be a compass that guides you toward economic literacy and enables you to navigate the complexities of financial systems with confidence and insight.

Basics of the American Economy

Welcome to an essential chapter that illuminates the heart of what powers the United States—the American economy. This foundation is not just about numbers and data; it's about understanding the spirit of innovation, hard work, and entrepreneurship that fuels the country. Let's embark on a journey to uncover how the U.S. economy functions, its significance, and what it means for you as an aspiring citizen.

At its core, the American economy is a mixed-market system, blending both private and public entities. This means while the government plays a crucial role in regulating and providing services, private enterprise dominates the economy, driven by the principles of freedom, competition, and innovation. This balance is key to fostering an environment where businesses can thrive and individuals can achieve the American Dream.

The concept of the "American Dream" is deeply intertwined with the economy. It's the idea that anyone, regardless of their background, can attain their own version of success through perseverance and hard work. This ethos is reflected in the opportunities the economy presents, from small businesses to large corporations, providing a platform for all to strive for prosperity.

Understanding the GDP, or Gross Domestic Product, is crucial. It's the total market value of all goods and services produced in the country and serves as a primary indicator of economic health. A growing GDP signifies an expanding economy, offering more opportunities for employment, investment, and improving standards of living. The U.S. economy, being one of the largest in the world, has a significant impact globally as well.

Inflation and unemployment rates are other vital metrics of economic performance. Inflation represents the rate at which the general level of prices for goods and services is rising, influencing the purchasing power of currency. Meanwhile, the unemployment rate measures the number of unemployed individuals actively seeking employment as a percentage of the labor force. Both indicators provide insights into the economy's current state and future outlook.

The Federal Reserve, the central banking system of the U.S., plays a pivotal role in managing the country's economic stability. It adjusts monetary policies to control inflation, influence unemployment rates, and support economic growth. Its decisions can impact everything from interest rates for loans and mortgages to the overall health of the financial markets.

Investment and savings are fundamental aspects of personal finance within the American economy. Investing in various assets like stocks, bonds, and real estate can grow wealth over time, offering financial security and opportunities. Saving, on the other hand, provides a safety net, ensuring individuals can support themselves in times of economic downturns or personal emergencies.

The labor market in the U.S. is dynamic, characterized by its resilience and adaptability. It's a place where different industries, ranging from technology to manufacturing, coexist and contribute to the country's economic diversity. This diversity is a strength, allowing the economy to remain robust even as certain sectors face challenges.

Entrepreneurship is at the heart of the American economy. With a supportive ecosystem that encourages innovation and risk-taking, the U.S. has seen the birth of many world-leading companies and technologies. This spirit of entrepreneurship underscores the importance of creativity, determination, and problem-solving in driving economic progress.

Trade is another pillar of the economy, with the U.S. being a major player on the global stage. It engages in importing and exporting goods and services worldwide, fostering international relations and economic partnerships. This global trade network not only enhances the domestic economy but also contributes to global economic stability.

The American economy is not without its challenges, including income inequality, healthcare, and environmental concerns. Addressing these issues is crucial for ensuring the economy works for everyone and sustains its growth in a way that is inclusive and responsible.

Education plays a crucial role in the economy by preparing a skilled workforce that can meet the demands of a rapidly changing market. From tech innovation to healthcare, educated individuals drive progress and maintain the U.S.'s competitive edge.

Lastly, the resilience of the American economy is notable. Through recessions and booms, the economy has shown a remarkable ability to recover and adapt. This resilience is powered by the collective effort of the government, businesses, and the American people, each playing a role in navigating challenges and seizing opportunities for growth.

As an aspiring citizen, understanding the basic workings of the American economy is fundamental. It's a framework that not only affects your daily life but also offers insights into the values of the nation: opportunity, innovation, and resilience. Embracing these concepts will not only help you in your journey towards citizenship but will also empower you to contribute to and thrive in this vibrant economy.

In conclusion, the American economy is a fascinating, complex system that provides a wealth of opportunities for those willing to learn and engage with it. As you continue your path to citizenship, take this understanding with you, knowing that in the American economy lies the potential to achieve your biggest dreams and aspirations. Your participation and contributions to this economy are valuable, and as you grow and succeed, so too does the nation.

The Role of Taxes and Personal Finance

Taxes and personal finance form the backbone of the economic understanding necessary to thrive in the US market. For many immigrants and individuals seeking US citizenship, mastering these components can significantly impact their American Dream. Taxes, at first glance, may seem like a daunting part of living in any new country. However, they play an essential role in funding public services and infrastructure, contributing to the overall well-being of society.

In the United States, the tax system operates on a federal, state, and sometimes local level, affecting income, purchases, property, and more. Understanding how taxes work is crucial not only for complying with the law but also for planning your financial future. It's a step towards financial empowerment, enabling you to make informed decisions about saving, investing, and spending.

Personal finance, on the other hand, is deeply personal and varies greatly from one individual to another. Managing your money effectively in the US involves budgeting, saving, investing, and managing debt. The financial decisions you make can either pave the way to financial security or lead to challenges that may hinder your ability to achieve your goals in your new home.

Let's start with the basics: budgeting. A budget is a plan that helps you track your income and expenses. Creating a budget allows you to see where your money is going, identify areas where you can cut back, and determine how much you can save or invest. It's a fundamental tool that can help you live within your means and save for future goals.

Saving is another critical aspect of personal finance. It's the process of setting aside money for future expenses, emergencies, or goals. In the US, various savings vehicles are available, each with its own set of rules and benefits. Understanding these options can help you make the most of your savings and achieve your financial goals more efficiently.

Investing is a way to potentially grow your savings over time. While it comes with risks, the US offers numerous investment opportunities, from stock markets to real estate. Educating yourself on these options, their risks, and potential returns can help you build a diversified portfolio that aligns with your financial objectives and risk tolerance.

Managing debt is equally important. In the US, credit is a powerful tool that, when used wisely, can help you build a financial foundation. However, mismanagement of debt can lead to financial strain. Learning how to use debt responsibly, understanding interest rates, and knowing the terms of your credit agreements can help you manage debt effectively.

Taxes and personal finance are interlinked. The way you manage your finances can impact your tax situation. For instance, certain investments and savings accounts offer tax advantages that can reduce your overall tax liability. Understanding these nuances can help you make more informed financial decisions.

Education is key to mastering taxes and personal finance. Thankfully, the US offers numerous resources to help individuals learn about these topics. From online courses and workshops to financial advisors and tax professionals, support is available to help you navigate the complex world of US taxes and personal finance.

Motivation plays a crucial role in managing your personal finances successfully. It requires discipline, planning, and a commitment to your financial goals. The journey may seem overwhelming at first, but with the right mindset and resources, you can achieve financial stability and independence.

Inspiration can be found in stories of individuals and families who have successfully navigated the complexities of the US financial system to achieve their American Dream. These stories highlight the importance of perseverance, education, and smart financial planning in overcoming challenges and achieving success.

Ultimately, understanding the role of taxes and personal finance is vital for anyone looking to build a successful life in the United States.

It's not just about complying with the law or managing your money; it's about empowering yourself to make informed decisions that align with your values and goals. As you embark on this journey, remember that education, motivation, and inspiration are your allies in achieving financial literacy. By embracing these principles, you open doors to opportunities and pave the way for a prosperous future in your new home.

As you continue to explore the vast landscape of the US market, keep in mind that financial literacy is a continuous journey. The economic environment evolves, and staying informed is crucial. Engaging with financial institutions, utilizing educational resources, and seeking advice from professionals are steps you can take to stay ahead in your financial journey.

In conclusion, the role of taxes and personal finance in the US market cannot be overstated. They are foundational elements that support individuals in achieving their goals and contributing to the prosperity of the society at large. As you move forward, let this knowledge empower you to make choices that align with your American Dream. Embrace the journey, commit to continuous learning, and watch as your financial understanding turns dreams into reality.

CHAPTER 11:
PREPARING FOR THE USCIS CIVICS
TEST

As you edge closer to the pinnacle of your journey towards becoming a U.S. citizen, the USCIS Civics Test stands as a crucial milestone. This chapter is meticulously crafted to equip you for this significant step. Understanding that this test is not just a formality but a rite of passage into the American civic body, we delve into effective study strategies that cater to various learning styles. We introduce an array of resources that are both informative and engaging, ensuring you have a well-rounded comprehension of U.S. history, government, and civic responsibilities. The essence of this chapter is confidence building, empowering you with knowledge and skills to face the test with assurance. Through sample questions and answers, we simulate the test environment, providing a clear expectation of what you'll encounter, thereby demystifying the test process. Additionally, valuable tips for test day emphasize practical preparations and mindset strategies, ensuring you're not just academically ready but also psychologically poised. This chapter is a beacon of guidance, illuminating the path to achieving not only a successful test outcome but also a deeper connection with the principles and ideals of your soon-to-be homeland.

Study Strategies and Resources

Embarking on the journey to pass the USCIS Civics Test is a commendable endeavor, one that requires dedication, strategy, and the right set of resources. In this section, we will explore a variety of study strategies and resources aimed at equipping you with the knowledge and confidence needed to excel. Consider this guide your ally in navigating the breadth of US history, government structure, and principles of democracy.

First and foremost, understand that a structured study schedule is your best friend. Divide your study time into manageable sections focusing on different topics covered in the test, such as American History, Government, and Civics. This approach not only prevents overwhelm but also ensures comprehensive coverage of the material.

Utilize official materials provided by the USCIS, starting with the '100 Civics Questions and Answers' document. This resource is indispensable as it gives you direct insight into the format and content of the actual test questions. Familiarize yourself with each question and answer, keeping in mind that understanding the concepts is far more beneficial than mere memorization.

Interactive learning tools such as online flashcards, practice tests, and educational videos can significantly enhance your retention. Websites like Quizlet provide free access to user-generated study sets on USCIS Civics Test topics, allowing you to test your knowledge and track your progress.

Incorporate review sessions into your study routine. Regular review sessions help cement your knowledge and identify any areas that might require more focus. Discussing topics with friends or members of study groups can also enhance understanding and memorize facts in a more engaging and memorable way.

Listening to podcasts and watching documentaries related to American history and government can provide contextual understanding and break the monotony of traditional study methods. These resources can offer insights into the significance of events and principles that have shaped the United States.

Leverage the power of educational apps designed for US citizenship test prep. Many of these apps present interactive quizzes, timed practice tests, and daily study reminders, making learning flexible and accessible from anywhere.

Consider attending citizenship classes offered by community centers or local NGOs. These classes can provide personalized instruction and the opportunity to ask questions and receive instant feedback from experienced educators.

Make reading a daily habit, starting with foundational documents such as the Constitution, Declaration of Independence, and Federalist Papers. Understanding these documents will not only aid in passing the test but enrich your appreciation for American values and governance.

Engage in community activities that relate to American history and government. Visiting historical sites, museums, and attending civic meetings can offer practical experiences and insights into the American way of life and governance.

Create a vision for yourself as an American citizen. Imagine participating in civic duties, understanding your rights, and contributing to your community. This mental practice can motivate and inspire you to engage deeply with your studies.

Practice speaking and writing about American history and government topics in English. This not only prepares you for the civics test but improves language skills crucial for the naturalization interview.

Remember, perseverance is key. At times, the volume of information may seem daunting, but with consistent effort and the right approach, passing the USCIS Civics Test is within your reach. Recognize each study session as a step closer to achieving your American dream.

Finally, explore online forums and social media groups where fellow test-takers share insights, advice, and encouragement. Learning from others' experiences can provide novel strategies and emotional support through this challenging yet rewarding journey.

In conclusion, while preparing for the USCIS Civics Test might seem like a daunting task, it's an achievable one with the right strategies and resources. Embrace the journey with an open heart and mind. Let the quest for knowledge about the United States empower you to become not just a test passer but an informed, engaged, and proud citizen of your new home country.

Sample Questions and Answers

Embarking on the journey to U.S. citizenship, it's crucial to not only memorize facts but to understand the spirit behind these questions you'll face on the USCIS Civics Test. This section has been meticulously crafted to mirror the actual test environment, presenting you with a curated selection of sample questions that range from the principles of American democracy to significant events in U.S. history. For each question, we provide detailed answers that aim to enrich your understanding of the U.S., preparing you not just for the test but for being an informed citizen. Imagine navigating through questions like "What is the supreme law of the land?" and understanding not just that the answer is "The Constitution," but grasping the essence of its principles such as liberty, equality, and justice. We've tailored this section to build your confidence, offering you strategies to tackle each query effectively. Through mastering these questions and answers, you're not just remembering facts; you're engaging with the very fabric of American society and taking a significant leap towards achieving your American dream.

Tips for Test Day Success

The path to US citizenship is a journey of personal growth, resilience, and dedication. As you approach the day of your USCIS Civics Test, know that you're about to cross a significant milestone. The preparation you've embarked on has not only been about memorizing facts but also understanding the fabric of the nation you're aspiring to call home. To ensure you arrive at test day feeling confident and prepared, we've compiled essential tips that capture the spirit of perseverance and success.

Firstly, it's crucial to acknowledge the hard work you've put into your test preparation. Remind yourself of the countless hours of study, the practice tests you've completed, and the knowledge you've gained about American history, government, and democratic principles. This mountain of effort is your foundation, and it's solid.

Secondly, understand the structure of the test and the format of the questions you will be asked. Familiarity breeds confidence. If you know what to expect, you're less likely to be caught off guard. This means taking the time to review sample questions available in study guides or the USCIS website. Embrace the types of questions, whether they're multiple choice, true/false, or require brief written responses.

On the night before your test, ensure you get a good night's sleep. Rest is just as crucial as study. Your brain needs time to consolidate all the knowledge you've gathered. A well-rested mind will serve you better than any last-minute cramming session.

Prepare your documents the evening before. Make a checklist of what you need to bring and gather everything in one place. Whether it's your green card, appointment letter, or any other required identification, having them ready will ease your mind and help you avoid a frantic search in the morning.

Mind your nutrition on the day of the test. Eat a healthy breakfast that will keep you energized and focused. Foods rich in omega-3 fatty acids, antioxidants, and vitamins can enhance cognitive function and memory. Avoid heavy, greasy foods that might make you feel sluggish.

Arrive early at the test center. Factor in extra time for unexpected delays. Arriving with time to spare will help you relax and mentally prepare, rather than rushing in at the last minute. Use this opportunity to take a few deep breaths, review your notes one last time, or simply center yourself.

Wear comfortable clothing to the test. While it's important to look presentable, you also want to ensure that discomfort doesn't distract you. Choose outfits that make you feel comfortable and confident.

During the test, manage your time wisely. Even though it's important to work diligently, don't rush through questions. Carefully read each one, consider your answers, and keep an eye on the clock. It's about finding the balance between being thorough and efficient.

Don't let difficult questions derail your confidence. It's normal to encounter a few questions that might seem more challenging. Instead of dwelling on them, move on and come back if time allows. Your goal is to answer as many questions correctly as possible.

Use elimination tactics if faced with multiple-choice questions. By removing answers you know are incorrect, you increase your chances of selecting the correct one. This strategy can be particularly useful if you find yourself unsure.

Pay attention to the instructions given by the test administrator. Carefully listen to or read any directions provided to avoid making unnecessary mistakes. If anything is unclear, don't hesitate to ask for clarification.

Remember to breathe. Anxiety and nerves are natural, but they don't have to control your test day. Practice deep breathing exercises to help calm your nerves before and during the test. A calm mind is a clear mind.

After completing your test, don't rush out. Take a moment to review your answers if time permits. Ensure you've answered every question and that you haven't made any obvious mistakes. Once you're satisfied, you can submit your test with confidence.

Lastly, approach your test day with a positive mindset. Visualize your success and the moment you pass. Believe in your preparation and yourself. Remember, this test is not just an assessment of your knowledge but a celebration of your journey and commitment to becoming a part of the American story. You've got this!

Implementing these tips on your test day will not only prepare you practically but also empower you mentally and emotionally. Each step you take brings you closer to achieving your American Dream. Remember, success on the USCIS Civics Test is not just about memorizing facts; it's about demonstrating your dedication to becoming a part of the United States' vibrant tapestry. Good luck, and see you at the finish line.

CHAPTER 12:
THE INTERVIEW AND BEYOND: FINAL STEPS TO CITIZENSHIP

The path to U.S. citizenship is both exhilarating and complex, culminating in the citizenship interview and, upon success, the Oath of Allegiance ceremony. This chapter unlocks the final barriers to becoming a full-fledged citizen, providing a road map for mastering the interview—a stage where your preparation, understanding, and dedication to the American values are put to the test. But it doesn't end at passing the interview; taking the Oath of Allegiance is a profound moment of commitment, not just a procedural step. Here, you symbolically and literally embrace the responsibilities and privileges of American citizenship, stepping into a role that millions have dreamt of and striven for. Beyond the ceremony, life as a new U.S. citizen opens up avenues for deeper civic engagement and personal growth. You are encouraged to continue exploring what it means to be an American, engaging with your community, and contributing to the nation's tapestry. This chapter is not just about crossing the finish line; it's about preparing you for the rich, ongoing journey of citizenship, ensuring that you're well-equipped to thrive and contribute to the United States with a full understanding of your rights and responsibilities.

Mastering the Citizenship Interview

The journey to U.S. citizenship is filled with hurdles, and one of the most significant is the citizenship interview. It's a pivotal moment that can shape your future. Understanding the intricacies of this interview and preparing adequately can transform this challenge into a stepping stone toward attaining your American Dream.

The citizenship interview is not just a formality; it's a comprehensive assessment designed to evaluate your knowledge of English and U.S. civics, as well as to verify the information you've provided in your application. It's your opportunity to demonstrate not only your readiness to become a U.S. citizen but also your commitment to the values and principles that define this nation.

Preparation is key to success. Begin with the end in mind and visualize yourself succeeding. This mental preparation boosts confidence and reduces anxiety. Review the materials provided by the USCIS, including the 100 civics questions and answers, and take advantage of study guides and practice tests. Immersing yourself in the English language through reading, writing, and conversation practice will also improve your proficiency and comfort level during the interview.

Understanding the format of the interview and what to expect can significantly ease your nerves. Typically, the interview is divided into three parts: a section to test your English proficiency through reading and writing simple sentences; a civics section where you'll be asked up to 10 questions from the list of 100, needing to answer at least 6 correctly; and a review of your N-400 application, where you'll be asked to confirm and clarify the details you submitted.

Remember, honesty is paramount. The officers are not only assessing your eligibility but also your character. If there are parts of your application that might raise questions—such as travel history or tax records—be prepared to discuss these openly. This honesty will serve you well in the long run.

Practice makes perfect. Enlist the help of friends or family members to conduct mock interviews. This practice can help you become more articulate in expressing your thoughts in English and provides a safe space to make mistakes, learn, and improve. Practicing under simulated interview conditions can alleviate stress and enhance your performance during the actual interview.

On the day of the interview, it's crucial to make a positive impression. Dress neatly and arrive early to allow yourself time to relax and focus. Bring all requested documents, including your appointment letter, permanent resident card, and any other documents that have been specifically requested in your interview notice. Missing documents can lead to delays or complications in your application process.

During the interview, listen carefully to the questions asked. If you don't understand a question, it's perfectly acceptable to ask for it to be repeated or rephrased. Speaking clearly and confidently will convey not only your language proficiency but also your preparedness and eagerness to become an American citizen.

It's important to view the citizenship interview as a conversation rather than an interrogation. The USCIS officer is there to assess, but also to assist. Approach the interview with a mindset of sharing your story and your aspirations of citizenship. Your genuine enthusiasm for becoming a part of the American fabric can stand out.

Post-interview, if you're approved, it's a cause for celebration, but remember, the journey doesn't end there. The completion of the interview brings you to the precipice of citizenship, the oath ceremony where your dream becomes reality. However, if there are areas for improvement or missing documentation, view it as an opportunity to address and excel. The USCIS may request additional documents or schedule a follow-up interview, so stay prepared and responsive.

Maintaining a positive outlook throughout the process is crucial. Encountering challenges or setbacks can be disheartening, but perseverance and a positive attitude can make all the difference. Remember, countless individuals have traversed this path to citizenship successfully. Their stories of success are a testament to the attainability of the American Dream through dedication and hard work.

Empower yourself with knowledge, preparation, and a positive mindset. This trifecta is your key to mastering the citizenship interview. It's not just about answering questions correctly but about demonstrating your readiness and resilience to become a contributing member of the American society.

In conclusion, the citizenship interview is a significant milestone on your journey to becoming a U.S. citizen. It's an opportunity to prove your commitment, knowledge, and character. With thorough preparation, honest communication, and a positive demeanor, you can navigate this process successfully. Remember, this interview is not just a hurdle but a stepping stone towards achieving your American Dream.

As you prepare for this pivotal step, keep sight of the bigger picture. Citizenship is not just a status but a privilege that comes with responsibilities and opportunities to contribute to the fabric of this nation. Embrace this journey with optimism and determination, and let your citizenship interview be a reflection of your readiness to be an active and engaged U.S. citizen.

The Oath of Allegiance Ceremony

Having surpassed the hurdles of applications, paperwork, and the citizenship interview, you now find yourself poised at the threshold of a transformative rite of passage: the Oath of Allegiance Ceremony. This pivotal event is not just a formality but a profound commitment to the United States, its Constitution, and its values. It is the culmination of your journey to American citizenship, marking your transition from immigrant to citizen, with all the rights, privileges, and responsibilities that entail.

The ceremony typically commences with a warm welcome from officials, recognizing the diverse origins of soon-to-be citizens, celebrating the unity amidst diversity that defines the fabric of American society. It is a moment steeped in significance, often charged with emotions for both the participants and their families, a tangible manifestation of dreams realized, sacrifices acknowledged, and futures reborn with new possibilities.

Before taking the Oath, candidates are usually called to stand and collectively recite the Pledge of Allegiance, a pledge to the flag and what it symbolizes. This act, simple yet profound, aligns the new citizens' fate with that of their adopted country, binding their diverse paths with a common pledge of allegiance and loyalty.

The core of the ceremony is, of course, the Oath of Allegiance itself. Administered by a designated official, this oath requires that you swear (or affirm) to absolutely and entirely renounce allegiance to any foreign sovereignty of whom or which you have been a subject or citizen; to support and defend the Constitution and laws of the United States against all enemies, foreign and domestic; to bear true faith and allegiance to the same; and to bear arms on behalf of the United States when required by law, or perform noncombatant service in the armed forces of the U.S. when required by law, or perform work of national importance under civilian direction when required by law.

It's not just the words but the solemn promise they encapsulate, committing oneself to the principles, responsibilities, and ideals of American citizenship. By taking this oath, you are pledging to be an active, engaged participant in the nation's democratic framework, ready to contribute to its ongoing story.

Following the Oath, a message from the President of the United States is often played or read, welcoming the new citizens into the American family. It is a powerful affirmation from the highest office in the land, recognizing the value and contributions of immigrants to the nation's strength and cultural richness.

Certificates of Naturalization are then distributed to the new citizens, serving as tangible proof of their U.S. citizenship. This document is crucial for many subsequent steps, such as applying for a U.S. passport, registering to vote, and facilitating the process of bringing family members to the United States.

The atmosphere of the ceremony is typically one of jubilation and pride, with families and friends often participating in the celebration. It's a moment when the barriers of origin melt away, and the common identity of being American comes to the forefront, highlighting the principle of e pluribus unum - out of many, one.

For many, the ceremony is an opportunity for reflection on the journey that brought them to this point, the hardships overcome, and the aspirations for the future. It is a time to acknowledge that while the path to citizenship may have been fraught with challenges, the strength, resilience, and determination displayed along the way are quintessentially American qualities.

Moreover, the ceremony signifies not an end but a beginning—the start of life as an American citizen with an active role in the democratic process. The right to vote, the freedom to express oneself, and the ability to pursue life's goals within the framework of American society are now fully yours to exercise.

Embrace the responsibilities that come with citizenship, including jury service, participating in the electoral process, and contributing to your community. These duties underscore the reciprocal nature of the rights and freedoms enjoyed.

Following the ceremony, many new citizens take the opportunity to register to vote, an act that underscores the democratic principle of civic participation. Voting is not just a right but a vital tool through which citizens have a say in the governance of their country. It's an empowering first act as a new citizen, symbolizing your voice in the American democratic process.

As the ceremony concludes and you step into the embrace of your fellow citizens, remember that American citizenship is a journey, not a destination. It's an ongoing commitment to grow, participate, and contribute to the tapestry of American life. Your unique heritage, perspectives, and experiences enrich the nation, and in turn, the realm of possibilities for what you can achieve and contribute expands infinitely.

Your citizenship is a testament to your resilience and determination, a badge of honor that speaks to your courage in pursuing the American dream. It's a significant achievement, but also the beginning of a new chapter where your dreams, aspirations, and contributions will continue to shape the identity and destiny of your adopted country.

The Oath of Allegiance Ceremony, therefore, is not just a formal obligation but a deeply personal commitment to the ideals of freedom, democracy, and opportunity that define the United States of America. It is an invitation to forge your path within the great American narrative, to contribute your voice to the chorus that shapes the nation's future. Welcome to your new beginning as a U.S. citizen.

Life as a New US Citizen

Congratulations, you've made it. After navigating the complex path to citizenship, taking the Oath of Allegiance signifies your official status as a US citizen. It's a moment of immense pride and a significant milestone in your journey. But what comes next? Life as a new US citizen is full of opportunities, responsibilities, and a chance to shape your destiny in your adopted homeland.

First and foremost, you have the right to vote, one of the most powerful tools in a democracy. Voting in local, state, and federal elections is not just a right; it's a privilege and a responsibility. It's your chance to influence policies, elect leaders, and make your voice heard on issues that matter to you and your community. Engage with the process, learn about the candidates and issues, and exercise your right to vote at every opportunity.

As a new citizen, you also have the opportunity to bring close family members to the United States. It's a chance to reunite with loved ones and provide them with opportunities for a better life. Understanding the process and requirements will be crucial, but your new status empowers you to open doors for your family like never before.

Embrace the diversity and freedoms of the United States. The US is a tapestry of cultures, languages, and beliefs. Participate in cultural exchanges, learn about different communities, and contribute your unique perspectives and traditions. It enriches the social fabric and deepens mutual understanding and respect among citizens from various backgrounds.

Your civic duties extend beyond voting. Jury duty is another responsibility of citizenship. It's a vital part of the judicial system, ensuring that the principle of being judged by one's peers is upheld. While it might seem cumbersome, serving on a jury is a profound civic honor and an opportunity to contribute to justice in your community.

Don't overlook the importance of community service. Volunteering offers a way to give back to your community, make a difference in the lives of others, and integrate more deeply into American society. Whether you're interested in education, the environment, or healthcare, there's a need for your time, talents, and passion.

Understanding your new rights is crucial. Familiarize yourself with the Constitution and the Bill of Rights, as these documents guarantee your liberties and protect you under the law. It's not just about knowing your rights; it's about understanding the legal framework that ensures those rights are respected and upheld.

Be aware of your tax responsibilities. Taxes fund public services, infrastructure, and the overall functioning of government. Filing your taxes correctly is both a duty and a necessity. It might seem daunting at first, but many resources are available to help you navigate this responsibility.

Explore personal finance and the US market. Understanding credit, mortgages, banking, and investing will empower you to make informed decisions about your finances. The American economy offers immense opportunities for growth and success, but navigating it requires knowledge and prudence.

Continuous education is key. The journey of learning about American history, society, and your rights as a citizen doesn't end with citizenship. Engage with community courses, online platforms, and books to further your understanding and appreciation of your new country.

Don't forget to update your Social Security record after becoming a citizen. This ensures that your work credits are accurately recorded and you're eligible for Social Security benefits when you retire.

As a new citizen, you can also apply for a US passport, a powerful document that facilitates international travel and serves as proof of your citizenship. It opens up a world of opportunities for work, study, and exploration abroad.

Contribute to the political process beyond voting. Consider running for office, supporting political campaigns, or engaging in activism. As a citizen, you have the right to shape policies and contribute to the political discourse in your community and beyond.

Lastly, celebrate your citizenship. It's a testament to your determination, hard work, and belief in the American dream. Share your journey with others, inspire future citizens, and take pride in your accomplishments. You are a vital part of the nation's future.

The journey to US citizenship is a transformative experience, marking the start of a new chapter in your life. Embrace the opportunities, fulfill your responsibilities, and contribute to the ongoing story of America. Your journey has equipped you with the understanding and skills to make a meaningful impact in your new country. Welcome to your new life as a US citizen.

CHAPTER 13:
KEEPING THE DREAM ALIVE:
CONTINUOUS LEARNING

The voyage towards US citizenship culminates not with the acing of a test or the solemnity of the Oath of Allegiance ceremony, but rather, with the embrace of a lifelong commitment to learning and civic engagement. This chapter underscores the essence of continuous learning as a cornerstone for thriving in a constantly evolving society. Equipping oneself with knowledge doesn't merely halt at achieving citizenship; it expands into realms that enrich personal growth and foster community welfare. The United States, with its rich tapestry of cultures and ceaseless drive for progress, provides fertile ground for ongoing education. From furthering one's understanding of American history to staying abreast of current events, continuous learning empowers citizens to actively participate in democracy, making informed decisions that reflect the best interests of both individuals and the collective. It lays out a roadmap for engaging in life-long learning opportunities, elucidating how staying informed and engaged ensures that the dream doesn't just stay alive but flourishes. By weaving together the myriad threads of personal development, community service, and the pursuit of knowledge, this chapter offers not just a vision but a call to action: to remain an ever-curious, ever-vigilant, and ever-active participant in the shaping of one's destiny and that of the United States.

Life-long Learning Opportunities

Embarking on the journey towards U.S. citizenship is a monumental step full of challenges and victories. However, the real journey begins after you've achieved this milestone. Living the American dream is an ongoing process that requires continuous learning and growth. The landscape of the world is ever-changing, and staying informed and adaptable is key to thriving in it. Life-long learning opportunities are abundant and can significantly contribute to your success and fulfillment in the United States.

Firstly, it's crucial to recognize that learning extends far beyond formal education. While pursuing degrees and certifications can open doors to new opportunities, the scope of learning encompasses so much more. The United States is a nation built on the foundation of continuous innovation and progress, which is reflected in its rich array of community colleges, universities, online courses, workshops, and seminars. These resources are invaluable for immigrants looking to expand their knowledge, skills, and professional networks.

Community colleges, in particular, are a fantastic resource for immigrants. They offer a variety of courses at relatively low costs and can serve as a stepping stone to higher education. Moreover, they are known for their supportive environments and resources tailored specifically to the needs of immigrant students, including ESL (English as a Second Language) programs. Engaging in these educational opportunities not only enhances your professional prospects but also aids in a smoother cultural integration.

Online learning platforms have emerged as a powerful tool for continuous education. Websites like Coursera, Udemy, and Khan Academy provide access to courses from some of the world's top universities for free or at a low cost. Whether you're looking to improve your English, learn computer programming, or understand American history more deeply, there's likely an online course that meets your needs. The flexibility of online learning allows you to balance education with work and family commitments.

Libraries are often overlooked sources of knowledge and learning in communities across the U.S. They offer more than just books; many libraries provide access to computers, internet, workshops, and classes on a range of topics including technology, business, and local history. They also offer special programs for children and adults, making them a valuable resource for the entire family. Libraries can play a crucial role in your lifelong learning journey, facilitating access to information and learning resources free of charge.

Mentorship and networking play a significant role in continuous learning and professional development. Building relationships with individuals who have navigated the path you're on can provide invaluable insights and guidance. Many cities have organizations and clubs that facilitate networking opportunities for professionals. Engaging with these communities not only expands your knowledge but also your support system in the U.S.

Volunteering is another powerful way to engage in lifelong learning. It provides practical experience, helps to build your professional network, and increases your understanding of the local community and culture. Many organizations and non-profits in the U.S. welcome the support of volunteers and provide opportunities to learn new skills and work in diverse environments.

Understanding the economic framework and personal finance is also vital for immigrants. The U.S. has a complex financial system, and becoming proficient in managing finances, understanding credit, taxes, and investments is crucial. Many community organizations and banks offer workshops and seminars on financial literacy, which can help you make informed decisions about your economic well-being.

Another aspect of lifelong learning is staying informed about political and social issues. Active civic participation is not only a right but a responsibility of U.S. citizens. Engaging with local and national news, understanding issues, and participating in community discussions can contribute significantly to your role as an informed citizen.

For parents, engaging in the education of your children is a form of lifelong learning that benefits the whole family. The U.S. education system may be different from what you're accustomed to, and becoming involved can help you navigate and support your children's educational journey. Schools often need volunteers and offer a variety of programs to help parents get involved.

Lifelong learning also encompasses the exploration of culture and history, which can enrich your understanding of your new home. Museums, historical sites, theaters, and cultural festivals are wonderful resources for immersive learning experiences that can deepen your connection to the community and country.

Finally, never underestimate the power of curiosity and an open mind. Lifelong learning is a mindset that sees every day as an opportunity to learn something new. It's about embracing change, seeking out new challenges, and viewing failures as learning experiences. This attitude will not only help you adapt to life in the U.S. but will also empower you to thrive and contribute to your community in meaningful ways.

In conclusion, life-long learning opportunities are abundant and varied in the United States. They provide a pathway for not just surviving but thriving in a new country. Education, mentorship, volunteering, and civic engagement are just a few avenues through which immigrants can continuously grow and contribute to their communities. Embracing the journey of continuous learning is integral to keeping the American dream alive for yourself and future generations.

To sum up, the journey towards and beyond U.S. citizenship is an adventure of continuous growth and learning. By taking advantage of the myriad opportunities for education and engagement available, you can ensure that you not only adapt and succeed in your new country but also lead a fulfilling and enriched life. The American dream is very much alive and within reach for those who commit to lifelong learning and exploration.

Staying Informed and Engaged Citizen

Embarking on the journey to becoming a U.S. citizen is a significant milestone. But what comes after the oath of allegiance is equally crucial. Citizenship isn't just a status; it's an ongoing commitment to being an informed and engaged member of the American community. This section explores how you can keep the dream alive, continuously learning and participating in the civic life of this great nation.

The fabric of American society is woven with the threads of diverse opinions, cultures, and voices. Staying informed means tuning into this rich tapestry, understanding different perspectives, and keeping abreast of local, national, and international news. It's about recognizing the impact of policies and decisions on the community and the world at large. In today's digital age, there's a wealth of information at your fingertips. Be selective with your sources to ensure you're getting accurate and balanced news.

Being an engaged citizen also involves understanding the political climate and how government actions reflect and impact societal values. Voting isn't the only way to have your voice heard. Engaging in community dialogues, attending town hall meetings, and connecting with your representatives are all ways to influence change and contribute to the decision-making process.

Volunteering is another powerful avenue for engagement. It's not only a way to give back but also to deeply connect with your community and understand its needs. Whether it's mentoring youth, helping at a local food bank, or participating in environmental clean-ups, volunteering can broaden your perspective and enrich your experience as a U.S. citizen.

Education plays a pivotal role in staying informed and engaged. Continuous learning opportunities abound, from community colleges offering courses on American history and government to libraries hosting talks and workshops. These resources can deepen your understanding of the nation's foundations and its dynamic society.

The Internet is a treasure trove of resources for those looking to expand their knowledge. MOOCs (Massive Open Online Courses) on a variety of subjects related to American culture, government, and history are available for free or at a low cost. This online accessibility makes it easier than ever to continue your education and become a more informed citizen.

Discussing and debating issues respectfully is another cornerstone of engagement. It's important to listen to others, even if you disagree, and express your opinions thoughtfully. These conversations can take place anywhere, from family dinners to online forums, and are vital for a healthy democracy.

Staying informed also means being critical of the information you consume. In an era where misinformation can spread rapidly, developing critical thinking and media literacy skills is essential. Learn to question and verify facts before sharing or acting on information.

Embracing the full rights and responsibilities of citizenship will enrich not only your life but also the fabric of American society. Your unique background and perspective can contribute to the nation's ongoing dialogue and development. Remember, America is a country built on the principle of progress, continuously shaped by its citizens.

Stay curious and open-minded. The more you learn about the U.S., its history, and its systems, the more empowered you'll be to participate fully in its democracy. This journey doesn't have an end point but rather is a continuous path of growth and participation.

Connect with local and national civic organizations. These groups can provide not only avenues for involvement and volunteerism but also forums for education and discussion. They offer a gateway to becoming a more active participant in the civic life of your community and country.

Celebrate your heritage while embracing your new identity as an American. Engagement doesn't mean leaving behind your roots. In fact, sharing your cultural heritage and learning about others can enhance mutual understanding and respect in the diverse mosaic that is the U.S.

Looking forward, the role of technology in civic engagement will only grow. Familiarize yourself with the digital tools and platforms that facilitate political activism, community service, and civic education. From apps that remind you of election dates to platforms that connect you with volunteer opportunities, technology can amplify your impact as a citizen.

Lastly, involve the next generation in civic activities. Whether it's discussing current events at home, participating in community service together, or attending civic ceremonies, fostering a sense of citizenship in young people is vital for the future of democracy.

Being an informed and engaged citizen is a profound way to honor the journey you've undertaken to become a part of this country. It's how you keep the dream alive, not just for yourself but for future generations. Your voice, your actions, and your dedication to learning can help shape a brighter future for all.

Realizing the American Dream

The journey towards realizing the American Dream is one filled with challenges, sacrifices, and immense rewards. It is a path that millions have traversed, each with their unique stories of aspiration and determination. This dream, deeply rooted in the heart of American history and civics, is not merely about the destination but also about the journey itself.

The dream of making a life in the United States is as old as the nation itself. From its founding pillars of liberty and democracy to the dynamic tapestry of its society, the United States has always symbolized a beacon of hope and opportunity. As you stand on the threshold of becoming a part of this great nation, it's essential to reflect on the values and responsibilities that shape its character.

Understanding the path to US citizenship is just the beginning. By engaging with the eligibility criteria, the naturalization process, and the USCIS, you've taken essential steps towards securing your place in the American tapestry. Each stage of the process, from obtaining a Green Card to mastering the civics test, is a step closer to your goal.

The history of the United States is a compelling narrative of resilience and innovation. From the early days of colonization to the birth of a nation built on independence and freedom, its history offers invaluable lessons for all aspiring citizens. These stories are not just about the past; they are a reminder of the enduring spirit that defines the American identity.

At the core of the United States are the principles of democracy. The Constitution and the Bill of Rights are not just documents but living promises of freedom, justice, and equality. Understanding these principles will deepen your appreciation of what it means to be an American citizen and the role you play in sustaining these ideals.

The American government's structure, with its division into the executive, legislative, and judicial branches, embodies the balance of power essential to democracy. Engaging with this system, from the intricacies of Congress to the significance of the Supreme Court, is part of your journey as a participant in American democracy.

The election process and citizenship go hand in hand. Voting rights, understanding the electoral system, and recognizing the importance of civic participation are crucial elements of citizenship. Engaging in the democratic process is one of the most profound ways to exercise your rights and contribute to the nation's future.

As citizens, we are endowed with rights and responsibilities. Freedom, protection, civic duties, and volunteering shape not just our community but our personal character as well. These aspects of citizenship encourage us to contribute positively and become active members of our communities.

America's symbols and landmarks, from the flag to the Statue of Liberty, are not just markers on a map; they are symbols of freedom and democracy. Understanding their significance helps connect us to the greater narrative of the nation and instills a sense of pride and belonging.

The insight into American society offered throughout this guide highlights the importance of cultural diversity, education, and social issues. This understanding fosters mutual respect and encourages us to be active, informed citizens. The fabric of American society is strengthened by its diversity and our contributions to it.

Economic understanding is also a critical component of realizing the American Dream. Grasping the basics of the American economy, the role of taxes, and personal finance is essential for prosperity and security. This knowledge empowers you to make informed decisions that contribute to your success in this country.

Preparing for the USCIS Civics Test and mastering the citizenship interview are fundamental steps in your journey. These steps not only require dedication but also an understanding of American history, government, and society. Success in these areas reflects not just your readiness for citizenship but your commitment to being an informed and engaged member of the American community.

As you take the Oath of Allegiance, remember that this is not the end of your journey but the beginning of a new chapter. Citizenship marks a significant milestone, but the process of integrating into American society continues. The dream does not stop at obtaining citizenship; it evolves into living as an engaged, informed, and proactive citizen.

Keeping the dream alive requires continuous learning and participation. Staying informed about civic issues, engaging in your community, and understanding the ongoing political and social changes are vital. The American Dream is an ever-evolving goal that demands our attention, participation, and dedication.

In conclusion, realizing the American Dream is a multifaceted journey that extends beyond citizenship. It's about embracing the values, responsibilities, and opportunities that define the United States. As you embark on this journey, remember that it's the spirit, hard work, and commitment to the common good that will shape your path. The dream is not just a destination but a continuous pursuit—of liberty, opportunity, and a better life for all.

Appendix A:
Key Documents and Speeches in American History

As you journey towards becoming a U.S. citizen, it's essential to immerse yourself in the rich tapestry of American history. This appendix is designed to guide you through some of the most pivotal documents and speeches that have shaped the nation. These pieces are not just words on paper; they are the backbone of American principles and values, echoing the aspirations, struggles, and ideals of the people and leaders who built America.

The Declaration of Independence (1776)

This foundational document marks the beginning of a new nation based on the principles of freedom, equality, and the pursuit of happiness. Crafted by Thomas Jefferson and signed by representatives from the 13 colonies, it asserts the colonies' right to break free from British rule. Its eloquent prose and powerful message make it a testament to the human spirit's desire for liberty.

The Constitution of the United States (1787)

The Constitution is the supreme law of the land, establishing the framework of the federal government and outlining the rights and freedoms of its citizens. Its first three words, "We the People," embody the democratic principle that government derives its power from the governed. This living document, including its 27 amendments, continues to guide and govern American life.

The Bill of Rights (1791)

The first ten amendments to the Constitution, known collectively as the Bill of Rights, guarantee essential freedoms and protections. These include freedom of speech, religion, and the press; the right to bear arms; and protection against unreasonable searches and seizures, among others. They form the cornerstone of American civil liberties.

The Federalist Papers (1787-1788)

A series of 85 essays written by Alexander Hamilton, James Madison, and John Jay, promoting the ratification of the U.S. Constitution. These articles provide insight into the framers' thoughts and the philosophy behind the Constitution's creation. They are a crucial resource for understanding the intentions of America's founders.

The Gettysburg Address (1863)

In the midst of the Civil War, President Abraham Lincoln delivered this brief but profound speech at the dedication of the Soldiers' National Cemetery in Gettysburg, Pennsylvania. In just over two minutes, Lincoln reaffirmed the principles of equality enshrined in the Declaration of Independence and proclaimed the Civil War as a struggle for the preservation of the Union that would bring about a "new birth of freedom."

Letter from Birmingham Jail (1963)

Written by Dr. Martin Luther King Jr. during his imprisonment for participating in civil rights protests, this letter is a powerful defense of nonviolent resistance to racism. It challenges not only the oppressors but also the white moderates and churches that remained silent in the face of injustice. Dr. King's eloquent call for equality, justice, and love is a defining document of the civil rights movement.

The Emancipation Proclamation (1863)

Issued by President Abraham Lincoln, this executive order declared the freedom of all enslaved persons in Confederate-held territory. Though it did not immediately free a single slave, it transformed the Civil War into a struggle for abolition and paved the way for the eventual end of slavery in the United States.

These documents and speeches are more than historical artifacts; they're living expressions of America's enduring ideals. As you study them, you'll gain a deeper appreciation for the principles of freedom, democracy, and equality that are at the heart of the American experience. This understanding will not only prepare you for the USCIS civics test but also inspire you to contribute to the ongoing story of the United States as its newest citizens.

APPENDIX B:
HELPFUL RESOURCES AND CONTACT
INFORMATION FOR IMMIGRANTS

Welcome to Appendix B, a curated list of resources and contact information designed to support you on your journey toward US citizenship. We understand the hurdles and challenges you might face along the way. Thus, we've compiled this guide to provide extra support, guiding you toward helpful resources that can make your path smoother and more informed. Whether you're looking for legal advice, language learning resources, or community support, this list is a starting point to finding the help you need.

Government Resources

- **United States Citizenship and Immigration Services (USCIS)**: The USCIS is the primary government agency overseeing lawful immigration to the United States. Their website offers comprehensive information on citizenship, including application forms and study materials for the civics test. For more information, visit *www.uscis.gov* or contact their National Customer Service Center at 1-800-375-5283.

- **Department of State (DOS)**: The DOS Bureau of Consular Affairs provides information on visa requirements for entering the U.S. and services for citizens abroad. Their website is a valuable resource for immigration processes at *travel.state.gov*.

Educational Resources

- **USA Learns**: A free website providing English language courses and information for immigrants adjusting to life in the United States, including preparation for the citizenship test. Access their resources at *www.usalearns.org*.

- **Adult Education and Literacy Programs**: Many local community colleges and community centers offer classes in English as a Second Language (ESL), civics, and preparation for the naturalization interview and test. Check your local community center or educational institutions for more information.

Legal Assistance

- **American Immigration Lawyers Association (AILA)**: A professional legal association of more than 15,000 attorneys and law professors who practice and teach immigration law. For referrals to qualified immigration lawyers, visit *www.ailalawyer.com*.

- **Immigration Advocates Network (IAN)**: Offers a national online network of legal advocates working on behalf of immigrants. IAN also provides a directory of non-profit immigration legal services at *www.immigrationadvocates.org/nonprofit/legaldirectory*.

Community Support

- **National Immigrant Justice Center**: Provides comprehensive legal services to low-income immigrants, refugees, and asylum seekers. They also advocate for human rights and immigration reform. Visit their site at *www.immigrantjustice.org*.

- **Immigrant Welcome Centers**: Scattered across the country, these centers offer newcomers a range of support services, from employment assistance to community integration programs. Search online for a welcoming center near you.

Cultural Integration

- **Local Community Centers and Libraries**: These are great places to connect with community events, cultural integration programs, and other resources that help immigrants feel at home in their new country.

- **Cultural Exchange Programs**: Engaging in cultural exchange programs can be a rewarding way to learn about American culture while sharing your own. Local universities and community organizations are good places to start exploring these opportunities.

Motivation and Support

Moving to a new country can be one of the most challenging experiences in life, but it's also one of the most rewarding. Remember, every step you take brings you closer to realizing your American Dream. Surround yourself with supportive people, reach out for help when you need it, and never lose sight of your goals. You're not alone on this journey, and the above resources can offer guidance, support, and community as you navigate the complex process of becoming a U.S. citizen. Keep moving forward with determination, resilience, and hope.

In closing, we encourage you to make the most of these resources. They're here to support you in becoming an informed, engaged, and empowered part of the diverse tapestry that is the United States. Welcome to your journey toward American citizenship — may it be successful and fulfilling.

Appendix C:
USCIS Civics Test Updates and Revisions

The journey to U.S. citizenship is both exhilarating and demanding, encapsulating not only the dreams and aspirations of individuals but also the embodiment of resilience. The USCIS civics test is a milestone on this journey, a culmination of preparation, understanding, and the embrace of American values and history. It is essential, therefore, to stay informed about the latest updates and revisions to the USCIS Civics Test to ensure readiness and confidence on test day.

Understanding the Significance of Updates

First and foremost, recognizing the importance of USCIS civics test updates is pivotal. These modifications are not just arbitrary changes but are reflective of evolving national priorities, historical milestones, and the continuous growth of the nation's identity. They ensure the test remains relevant and an accurate measure of an applicant's understanding of U.S. civics.

Categories of Revisions

- **Content Updates:** These alterations include the addition, deletion, or modification of test questions to reflect the current state of U.S. government, history, and civics knowledge. It's vital to keep abreast of these changes to avoid studying outdated information.

- **Format Adjustments:** At times, the structure of the test may undergo modifications to enhance its accessibility or comprehensiveness. Familiarity with the test format is crucial for efficient preparation and managing test-day expectations.

- **Scoring Criteria:** Understanding any adjustments to how responses are evaluated can significantly influence study strategies and test performance. Clear knowledge of the scoring rubric enables focused preparation.

Staying Informed

To stay updated with the USCIS Civics Test revisions:

- Regularly visit the *Official USCIS website*. It is the primary source of authoritative and current information regarding the civics test.

- Engage with community support organizations. They often offer workshops, study groups, and resources aligned with the latest test guidelines.

- Utilize approved study materials. Ensure any preparation books, online resources, or classes are based on the most recent test version.

Embracing the Evolution

The changes to the USCIS Civics Test are a reflection of the nation's journey, encapsulating its ever-evolving history, governance, and societal values. Approaching these updates with enthusiasm and an eagerness to learn is not only beneficial for test preparation but also fosters a deeper appreciation and understanding of what it means to be a U.S. citizen.

Remember, the journey to citizenship is a learning experience, empowering you with knowledge that transcends the test. As you navigate through these updates and embrace the rich tapestry of American life and governance, let your preparation be guided by curiosity, determination, and a vision of success. Your path to citizenship is a testament to your resilience and commitment to being part of the American dream, and staying informed and adaptive to these revisions is a crucial step in achieving that dream.

GLOSSARY OF TERMS RELATED TO US CITIZENSHIP

Embarking on the journey towards US citizenship is an adventure filled with learning and discovery. Understanding the vocabulary and concepts related to this process is foundational to success. This glossary is designed to illuminate and empower you, compiling key terms that are essential for navigating the pathways to citizenship. Embrace this adventure with confidence and curiosity.

A

- **Alien** - Any person not a citizen or national of the United States.

- **Amendment** - A modification to the U.S. Constitution; the first ten amendments are known as the Bill of Rights.

- **Asylum** - Protection granted to foreign nationals who can't return to their home country due to persecution or a well-founded fear of persecution based on race, religion, nationality, political opinion, or membership in a particular social group.

B

- **Bill of Rights** - The first ten amendments to the Constitution, guaranteeing fundamental rights and protections to American citizens.

- **Biometrics** - Unique physical characteristics, such as fingerprints, used for identification purposes, often collected during the citizenship and naturalization process.

C

- **Citizenship** - The status of being a legal member of a country, with specific rights, duties, and benefits.

- **Civics Test** - An examination that aspiring citizens must pass, covering U.S. history and government, to demonstrate their knowledge and understanding of foundational American principles.

- **Constitution** - The supreme law of the United States, outlining the national framework of government and individual rights.

D

- **Democracy** - A form of government in which power is vested in the people, who rule either directly or through freely elected representatives.

- **Deportation** - The formal removal of a foreign national from the U.S. for violating immigration laws.

- **Dual Citizenship** - The simultaneous holding of citizenship in two countries.

E

- **Eligibility** - Suitability based on set conditions or requirements; in the context of US citizenship, it refers to the criteria that must be met to apply for naturalization.

- **Expedited Naturalization** - A faster process for certain applicants to become US citizens, available under specific conditions.

F

- **Federalism** - The division of power between the national government and the states.

- **First Amendment** - Part of the Bill of Rights that guarantees freedoms concerning religion, expression, assembly, and the right to petition.

G

- **Green Card** - Informal name for the card showing that a person has lawful permanent resident status in the United States.

I

- **Immigrant** - A person who comes to a country to take up permanent residence.

- **INS** (Immigration and Naturalization Service) - Former U.S. agency that was responsible for immigration and naturalization, succeeded by USCIS.

- **Integration** - The process of becoming a full and equal part of American society.

J

- **Judiciary** - The judicial branch of the U.S. government, responsible for interpreting laws.

N

- **Naturalization** - The legal process through which a foreign citizen or national can become a U.S. citizen.
- **Naturalization Test** - See Civics Test.

O

- **Oath of Allegiance** - A pledge that must be taken by all individuals wishing to become U.S. citizens through naturalization. The oath signifies the new citizen's loyalty and allegiance to the United States.

P

- **Permanent Resident** - See Green Card.
- **Permanent Resident Card** - Official name for the documentation also known as a Green Card, which confirms the bearer's authorization to live and work in the United States permanently.

R

- **Refugee** - A person who has been forced to leave their country in order to escape war, persecution, or natural disaster.
- **Rule of Law** - The principle that all people and institutions are subject to and accountable to law that is fairly applied and enforced.

S

- **States' Rights** - The rights and powers held by individual US states rather than by the federal government.

- **Supreme Court** - The highest court in the United States, with ultimate appellate jurisdiction and the authority to interpret the Constitution.

U

- **USCIS** (United States Citizenship and Immigration Services) - The government agency that oversees lawful immigration to the United States, including the naturalization process.

While this glossary presents a concise overview, the journey to citizenship is rich with opportunities for deeper exploration. Embrace each term and concept not just as a step toward passing a test, but as a stepping stone towards a meaningful engagement with your new homeland. Let this knowledge be the light guiding you through the rewarding pathway to becoming a citizen of the United States. Your commitment and enthusiasm are pivotal to this inspirational venture. Welcome to your next chapter.

Online Review Request for This Book

If you found this book a valuable companion on your journey towards understanding and achieving US citizenship, we'd be honored if you could take a moment to leave us a review online; your insights can empower others in similar journeys and help us enhance this guide for future readers.

www.ingramcontent.com/pod-product-compliance
Lightning Source LLC
Chambersburg PA
CBHW051419280526
45785CB00003B/1077